"Age doesn't matter unless you're a cheese."

Wisdom *from* Our Elders

by Kathryn *and* Ross Petras

WORKMAN PUBLISHING • NEW YORK

Cataloging and publication information is available from
the Library of Congress
ISBN-13: 978-0-7611-2518-1
ISBN-10: 0-7611-2518-3

Workman books are available at special discounts when
purchased in bulk for premiums and sales promotions as well
as for fund-raising or educational use. Special editions or
book excerpts can also be created to specification. For details,
contact the Special Sales Director at the address below.

Workman Publishing Company, Inc.
708 Broadway
New York, NY 10003-9555
www.workman.com

Printed in the United States of America
First printing March 2002

15 14 13 12 11

To the memories of our grandparents, Spiros and Kalliope Petras and Peter and Marika Leopold

Yes, it's true. We are getting older.

For some, the passage of time is a blessing, to others a curse, but for all of us aging is a reality we can't escape. We can moan about it, we can accept it, or we can choose to celebrate the wisdom and perspective that so often go hand in hand with experience.

And that's the reason for this book. Since there *is* a lot to be said for getting older, we decided to collect some of the best things that *have* been said. Our thought was that all of us—whether we're young or old or anywhere in between—could pick up pointers from people who have been there, done that. We began by reading dozens upon dozens of autobiographies and biographies, and then we pored over letters and collections of quotations. We ended up with entries by several hundred people who were, in many cases, as different as different can be. But they had two things in common: They were over the age of sixty when they said the words we've included here. And they had something to say.

Collectively, these people have done it all. They've painted pictures, diapered babies, climbed mountains, watched baseball games (and played in them), built businesses, lived life. And because they've been generous enough to share their experiences and insights, their words come together to form a book that offers both inspiration and guidance: a manual for living well from people who have done just that. When they grapple with the big issues—death, immortality, love—we do, too. When they look back at their relationships, we can see our own friends and family anew. And when they make us laugh, we can be grateful.

We truly enjoyed compiling this collection. For a while, we practically lived with some of the people quoted here, and found we liked most of them. Federico Fellini's quirkiness prompted us to go out and rent a few of his films. Jimmy Carter's humanism prompted us to reevaluate his presidency. Albert Einstein's wit and sense of social responsibility made us realize how much more there is to a mathematician or scientist than a set of abstruse equations. And, of course, actress Billie Burke's observation that "age doesn't matter, unless you are a cheese" gave us a title for our book.

Like death and taxes, growing older is an inevitability. But as the voices in this book remind us, some inevitabilities are a whole lot more positive than others.

❦ KATHRYN AND ROSS PETRAS
NEW YORK CITY

I suppose real old age begins when one looks backward rather than forward.

❦ WRITER MAY SARTON

As a grandfather, I'm entitled to a few words of advice to the young, based upon my long and unvarying experience as a transgressor. I can sum them up with these answers to the oft-repeated question, "What would you do or not do if you had it all to do over again?"

I would spend more time with my children.

I would make my money before spending it.

I would learn the joys of wine instead of hard liquor.

I would not smoke cigarettes when I had pneumonia.

I would not marry the fifth time.

❦ DIRECTOR/ACTOR JOHN HUSTON

What a wonderful life I've had! I only wish I'd realized it sooner.

❦ WRITER COLETTE

For the past eighty years, I have started each day in the same manner. It is not a mechanical routine but something essential to my daily life. I go to the piano, and I play two preludes and fugues of Bach. I cannot think of doing otherwise. It is a sort of benediction on the house. But that is not its only meaning for me. It is a rediscovery of the world of which I have the joy of being a part. It fills me with awareness of the wonder of life, with a feeling of the incredible marvel of being a human being.

❦ MUSICIAN PABLO CASALS

Security is mostly superstition. . . .
Avoiding danger is no safer in the long run than outright exposure. Life is either a daring adventure, or nothing.

❦ WRITER/LECTURER HELEN KELLER

There are dreams of love, life, and adventure in all of us. But we are also sadly filled with reasons why we shouldn't try. These reasons seem to protect us, but in truth they imprison us. They hold life at a distance. Life will be over sooner than we think. If we have bikes to ride and people to love, now is the time.

❦ PSYCHIATRIST ELISABETH KÜBLER-ROSS

Train your will to concentrate on a limited objective. When young, you spread your effort over too many things. . . . If your try fails, what does it matter—all life is a failure in the end. The thing is to get sport out of trying.

❦ ADVENTURER SIR FRANCIS CHICHESTER, AFTER SAILING AROUND THE WORLD AT AGE SEVENTY-ONE

I have thousands of opinions still, but that is down from millions and, as always, I know nothing.

❦ WRITER HAROLD BRODKEY

There are only two ways to live your life. One is as though nothing is a miracle. The other is as though everything is a miracle.

❦ PHYSICIST ALBERT EINSTEIN

Age ... doesn't matter, unless you are a cheese.

❧ ACTRESS BILLIE BURKE

What is life? It is the flash of a firefly in the night. It is the breath of a buffalo in the wintertime. It is the little shadow which runs across the grass and loses itself in the sunset.

❦ LAST WORDS OF BLACKFOOT WARRIOR CROWFOOT

"The days of struggle are over," I should be able to say. "I can look back now and tell myself I don't have a single regret."

But I do.

Many years ago a very wise man named Bernard Baruch took me aside and put his arm around my shoulder. "Harpo, my boy," he said, "I'm going to give you three pieces of advice, three things you should always remember."

My heart jumped and I glowed with expectation. I was going to hear the magic password to a rich, full life from the master himself. "Yes, sir?" I said. And he told me the three things.

I regret I've forgotten what they were.

❦ COMEDIAN HARPO MARX

You make what seems
to be a simple choice:
Choose a man or a job
or a neighborhood—and
what you have chosen
is not a man or a job or
a neighborhood, but a life.

❦ WRITER JESSAMYN WEST

The present is the ever-moving shadow that divides yesterday from tomorrow. In that lies hope.

❦ ARCHITECT FRANK LLOYD WRIGHT

Each one must learn
for himself the highest
wisdom. It cannot be
taught in words. . . .
Men who work cannot
dream, and wisdom
comes to us in dreams.

❦ **WANAPUN (NATIVE AMERICAN) PROPHET SMOHALLA**

I don't care, frankly,
what people think.
I do what I like.

❦ CHEF JULIA CHILD

Never retire! Do what you do and keep doing it. But don't do it on Friday. Take Friday off. Friday, Saturday, and Sunday, do fishing, do sexual activities, watch Fred Astaire movies. Then from Monday to Thursday, do what you've been doing all your life, unless it's lifting bags of potatoes off the back of a truck. I mean, after eighty-five that's hard to do. My point is: Live fully and don't retreat.

❧ DIRECTOR/WRITER MEL BROOKS

It isn't for the moment
you are struck that you
need courage, but for
the long uphill climb
back to sanity and faith
and security.

❦ WRITER ANNE MORROW LINDBERGH

Carl Jung said that part of our struggle on earth is to recognize the royalty in ourselves. I think when we do, we can also recognize the royalty of others. That is the secret of "love thy neighbor as thyself."

We are all born of royalty, in a gold box, even a ragman's son. Within us is a tiny seed of godliness—the spirit of God, the Shechinah—and throughout our life we must learn to nourish it.

❦ ACTOR KIRK DOUGLAS

All is pattern,
all life, but we
can't always see
the pattern when
we are part of it.

❦ WRITER BELVA PLAIN

At eighty I believe I am a far more cheerful person than I was at twenty or thirty. I most definitely would not want to be a teenager again. Youth may be glorious but it is also painful to endure. Moreover, what is called youth is not youth; it is rather something like premature old age.

❦ WRITER HENRY MILLER

You know that I'm at death's door. But the trouble is that I'm afraid to knock.

❦ WRITER W. SOMERSET MAUGHAM

When I was very young, I thought about what old age would be like. It didn't seem very real. I assumed I would be exactly the same as I was then, except that I might have a long white beard like Father Christmas and not ever have to shave. I planned to eat whatever I wanted—mozzarella, pasta, rich desserts—and I would travel and see all the museums I never had the time to see before.

One day I looked into the mirror and thought, "Where did that old man come from?" Then I realized he was me, and all I wanted to do was work.

❦ DIRECTOR FEDERICO FELLINI

Aging seems to be the only available way to live a long life.

❦ COMPOSER DANIEL-FRANÇOIS-ESPRIT AUBER

When you get to the end
of all the light you know
and it's time to step into the
darkness of the unknown,
faith is knowing that one
of two things shall happen:
Either you will be given
something solid to stand on,
or you will be taught how
to fly.

❧ PHYSICIST EDWARD TELLER

You do what you can for as long as you can, and when you finally can't, you do the next best thing. You back up, but you don't give up.

❦ TEST PILOT GENERAL CHUCK YEAGER

I take a simple
view of living:
It is Keep your
eyes open and
get on with it.

❦ ACTOR LAURENCE OLIVIER

The secret of staying young is to live honestly, eat slowly, and lie about your age.

❦ COMEDIAN LUCILLE BALL

Here, with whitened hair, desires failing, strength ebbing out of him, with the sun gone down and with only the serenity and the calm warning of the evening star left to him, he drank to Life, to all it had been, to what it was, to what it would be. Hurrah!

❦ WRITER SEAN O'CASEY

It is high time
for me to depart,
for at my age
I now begin to
see things as they
really are.

❦ PHILOSOPHER LE BOVIER DE FONTENELLE

Worrying is the most
natural and spontaneous
of all human functions.
It is time to acknowledge
this, perhaps even to learn
to do it better.

❦ PATHOLOGIST LEWIS THOMAS

I cannot give you the
formula for success,
but I can give you
the formula for failure,
which is: Try to please
everybody.

❦ EDITOR HERBERT BAYARD SWOPE

Old age ain't for sissies.

❧ ACTRESS BETTE DAVIS

Nothing except possibly
love and death are of
importance, and even the
importance of death is
somewhat ephemeral,
as no one has yet faxed
back a reliable report.

❦ NATURALIST/WRITER GERALD DURRELL

If old age means a crown of thorns, the trick is to wear it jauntily.

❧ WRITER CLARE BOOTH LUCE

I don't know what I may
seem to the world, but,
as to myself, I seem to
have been only like a boy
playing on the sea shore,
and diverting myself in now
and then finding a smoother
pebble or a prettier shell
than ordinary, whilst the
great ocean of truth lay all
undiscovered before me.

❦ SCIENTIST ISAAC NEWTON

Men have one fatal flaw. It's the yearning for love and romance. And that longing for love outlasts the capacity for sex; it persists to old age.

❦ WRITER JOSEPH HELLER

I believe, not theoretically, but from direct personal experience, that very few of the things that happen to us are purposeless or accidental (and this includes suffering and grief—even that of others), and that sometimes one catches a glimpse of the link between these happenings. I believe—even when I myself am being blind and deaf, or even indifferent—in the existence of a mystery.

❦ WRITER IRIS ORIGO

There isn't anybody who doesn't like to see an old man make a comeback. Jimmy Connors seemed like a jerk to me until he was forty. After that, I rooted for him all the time. How could you not?

❧ FINANCIER T. BOONE PICKENS

I am almost sure to be blotted out by death, but sometimes I think it is not impossible that I may continue to live in some other manner after my physical death. I feel every suicide has that doubt: Is what I am going to do worthwhile? Will I be blotted out, or will I continue to live on in another world? Or, as Hamlet wonders, what dreams will come when we leave this body?

❦ WRITER JORGE LUIS BORGES

The love we have in our youth is superficial compared to the love that an old man has for his wife.

❧ HISTORIAN WILL DURANT

To get it right, be born with luck or else make it. *Never* give up. Get the knack of getting people to help you, and also pitch in yourself. A little money helps, but what *really* gets it right is *never*—I repeat—*never* under any condition face the facts.

❦ ACTRESS/WRITER RUTH GORDON

I live by one principle: Enjoy life
with no conditions! People say,
"If I had your health, if I had your
money, oh, I would enjoy myself."
It is not true. I would be happy if
I were lying sick in a hospital bed.
It must come from the inside.
That is the one thing I hope to
have contributed to my children,
by example and by talk: to make
no conditions, to understand that
life is a wonderful thing and to
enjoy it, every day, to the full.

❧ MUSICIAN ARTUR RUBINSTEIN

I learned that one can never go back, that one should not ever try to go back— that the essence of life is to go forward. Life really is a One Way Street.

❧ WRITER AGATHA CHRISTIE

Learning and sex until rigor mortis.

❦ ACTIVIST MAGGIE KUHN'S MOTTO

There is a delicate irony in the fact that my first wife introduced me to my second.

Irony or plan?

It is what each man must conclude for himself. As hard as he tried, this man cannot believe in divine intervention. And still he cannot credit everything to happenstance.

Somewhere there lies an answer.

I hope one day to find it.

❦ ACTOR EDWARD G. ROBINSON

A woman of ninety said to
M. de Fontenelle, then ninety-five,
"Death has forgotten us." "Shh,"
said M. de Fontenelle, putting his
finger to his lips.

❧ RELATED BY WRITER
SÉBASTIEN ROCH NICOLAS CHAMFORT

I have everything
now that I had
twenty years ago,
except now it's
all lower.

❦ STRIPPER GYPSY ROSE LEE

I can live with doubts and uncertainty
and not knowing. I think it's more
interesting to live not knowing than to
have answers which might be wrong. . . .
I don't feel frightened by not knowing
things, by being lost in a mysterious
universe without having any purpose,
which is the way it really is so far as
I can tell. It doesn't frighten me.

❦ PHYSICIST RICHARD P. FEYNMAN

Every human being on this earth is born with a tragedy... he's born with the tragedy that he has to grow up. He has lost everything that is lovely and must fight for a new loveliness of his own making, and it's a tragedy. A lot of people don't have the courage to do it.

❦ ACTRESS HELEN HAYES

All of us failed to match our dreams of perfection. So I rate us on the basis of our splendid failure to do the impossible.

❦ WRITER WILLIAM FAULKNER

Good days are to be gathered
like sunshine in grapes, to be
trodden and bottled into wine
and kept for age to sip at ease
beside the fire. If the traveler has
vintaged well, he need trouble
to wander no longer; the ruby
moments glow in his glass at will.

❦ WRITER FREYA STARK

Never have I enjoyed
youth so thoroughly as
I have in my old age.

❧ WRITER GEORGE SANTAYANA

The dominant
thought of youth
is the bigness of
the world, of age
its smallness.

❦ WRITER JOHN BUCHAN

Show me a good loser and I'll show you an idiot.

❦ BASEBALL MANAGER LEO DUROCHER

Work became more important to me as I grew older. When you are very young, there are competing pleasures. Maybe you need less to make yourself happy because everything is new to you. The world of old age is a shrinking world. Smaller things are magnified. It's like childhood. Few people are important to you, but they are *very* important. Little things get bigger. Food becomes more important. It is your work that makes you feel young, not your love affairs. After a certain point, your love affairs make you feel older.

❦ DIRECTOR FEDERICO FELLINI

I'm at the age where food has taken the place of sex in my life. In fact, I've just had a mirror put over my kitchen table.

❦ COMEDIAN RODNEY DANGERFIELD

I used to dread getting older because I thought I would not be able to do all the things I wanted to do, but now that I am older, I find that I don't want to do them.

❦ POLITICIAN LADY NANCY ASTOR

Never regret.
If it's good,
it's wonderful.
If it's bad,
it's experience.

❦ WRITER VICTORIA HOLT

In the greatest confusion there is still an open channel to the soul. It may be difficult to find because by midlife it is overgrown, and some of the wildest thickets that surround it grow out of what we describe as our education. But the channel is always there, and it is our business to keep it open, to have access to the deepest part of ourselves.

❦ WRITER SAUL BELLOW

As long as you
can admire and
love, then one is
young forever.

❦ MUSICIAN PABLO CASALS

Go out on a limb. That's where the fruit is.

❦ STATESMAN JIMMY CARTER

One of the delights
known to age, and
beyond the grasp
of youth, is that of
Not Going.

❦ WRITER J. B. PRIESTLEY

I have begun in old age to understand just how oddly we are all put together. We are so proud of our autonomy that we seldom, if ever, realize how generous we are to ourselves, and just how stingy with others. One of the booby traps of freedom—which is bordered on all sides by isolation—is that we think so well of ourselves. I now see that I have helped myself to the best cuts at life's banquet.

❦ WRITER SAUL BELLOW

Who says I am old?
Is an old man like this?
Heart welcomes sweet flowers,
Laughter floats over fragrant cups:
What can I do, what can I say?
My hoary hair floats in the spring
    wind.

❦ KOREAN POET KIM CHONG-GU

Nothing happens, and nothing happens, and everything happens.

❦ WRITER FAY WELDON

Death is the wake-up call, the unavoidable mandate, that makes enlightenment possible, and helps our souls to grow. This is why Plato, when asked on his deathbed for one final word of advice, responded to his pupils, "Practice dying."

❧ WRITER RAM DASS

One of the oddest things in life, I think, is the things one remembers.

❦ WRITER AGATHA CHRISTIE

Don't try to go too fast.
Learn your job. Don't ever
talk until you know what
you're talking about. . . .
If you want to get along,
go along.

❦ POLITICIAN SAM RAYBURN

Life is full of miracles,
but they're not always
the ones we pray for.

❦ ACTRESS EVE ARDEN

Literature has neglected
the old and their emotions.
The novelist never told
us that in life, as in other
matters, the young are just
beginners and that the art
of loving matures with age
and experience.

❦ WRITER ISAAC BASHEVIS SINGER

I used to have a sign over my computer that read OLD DOGS CAN LEARN NEW TRICKS, but lately I sometimes ask myself how many more new tricks I *want* to learn. Wouldn't it be easier just to be outdated?

❦ WRITER RAM DASS

INTERVIEWER:
To what do you
attribute your
longevity?

CHEF JULIA CHILD:
Red meat and gin.

I read a story once of a group of Jews who were escaping the Nazis. They were walking over a mountain, and they carried with them the sick and the old and the children. A lot of old people fell by the wayside and said, "I'm a burden; go on without me." They were told, "The mothers need respite, so instead of just sitting there and dying, would you take the babies and walk as far as you can?" Once the old people got the babies close to their bosom and started walking, they all went over the mountain. They had a reason to live.

❧ ACTRESS RUBY DEE

I am ready to meet my Maker. Whether my Maker is ready for the ordeal of meeting me is another matter.

❦ STATESMAN WINSTON CHURCHILL, IN A SPEECH ON HIS SEVENTY-FIFTH BIRTHDAY

I still have two abiding passions. One is my model railway, the other— women. But, at the age of eighty-nine, I find I am getting just a little too old for model railways.

❦ CONDUCTOR PIERRE MONTEUX

To me, life is like the back nine in golf. Sometimes you play better on the back nine. You may not be stronger, but hopefully you're wiser. And if you keep most of your marbles intact, you can add a note of wisdom to the coming generation.

❦ ACTOR/DIRECTOR CLINT EASTWOOD

Courage is
very important.
Like a muscle,
it is strengthened
by use.

❦ ACTRESS/WRITER RUTH GORDON

A man can do only
what a man can do.
But if he does that
each day, he can sleep
at night and do it again
the next day.

❦ MISSIONARY AND PHILOSOPHER
ALBERT SCHWEITZER

If the devil were to offer me a resurgence of what is commonly called virility, I'd decline. "Just keep my liver and lungs in good working order," I'd reply, "so I can go on drinking and smoking."

❦ DIRECTOR LUIS BUÑUEL

It's a funny thing about life; if you refuse to accept anything but the best, you very often get it. . . .

❧ WRITER W. SOMERSET MAUGHAM

I'm having a glorious old age. One of my greatest delights is that I have outlived most of the opposition.

❧ ACTIVIST MAGGIE KUHN

I always say—
that *everything*
is possessed of
infinity and
eternity. . . .

❦ MUSICIAN YEHUDI MENUHIN

The old know
what they want;
the young are sad
and bewildered.

❦ WRITER LOGAN PEARSALL SMITH

When I see nothing
annihilated, and not even
a drop of water wasted,
I cannot suspect the
annihilation of souls, or
believe that He will suffer
the daily waste of millions
of minds ready made that
now exist, and put Himself
to the continual trouble of
making new ones.

❦ STATESMAN BENJAMIN FRANKLIN

It isn't where you came from; it's where you're going that counts.

❧ SINGER ELLA FITZGERALD

When you're my age,
you just never risk
being ill—because
then everyone says,
"Oh, he's done for."

❦ ACTOR JOHN GIELGUD

Now that I am ninety-five years old,
looking back over the years, I have seen
many changes taking place. So many
inventions have been made; things now
go faster. In olden times, things were
not so rushed. I think people were more
content, more satisfied with life than
they are today. You don't hear nearly
as much laughter and shouting as you
did in my day, and what was fun for us
wouldn't be fun now. . . . In this age,
I don't think people are as happy; they
are worried. They're too anxious to
get ahead of their neighbors; they are
striving and striving to get something
better. I do think in a way that they have
too much now. We did with much less.

❦ ARTIST GRANDMA MOSES

The older one gets,
the more one feels
that the present
must be enjoyed;
it is a precious gift,
comparable to a state
of grace.

❦ SCIENTIST MARIE CURIE

Old age and the wear of time teach many things.

❦ PLAYWRIGHT SOPHOCLES

Trying to hang on to youth, trying to hang on to what was really great twenty years ago, throws you totally off. You've got to go with it and seek the *abundance* that's in the new thing. If you hang on to the old thing, you will not experience the new.

❦ SCHOLAR JOSEPH CAMPBELL

Perhaps one has to be ... old before one learns how to be amused rather than shocked.

❦ WRITER PEARL S. BUCK

Can one know one's self? Is one ever *somebody*? I don't know anything about it anymore. It now seems to me that one changes from day to day and that every few years one becomes a new being.

❦ WRITER GEORGE SAND

You're never too old to become younger.

❧ ACTRESS MAE WEST

Even death is unreliable; instead of zero it may be some ghastly hallucination, such as the square root of minus one.

❦ WRITER SAMUEL BECKETT

From birth to eighteen,
a girl needs good parents.
From eighteen to thirty-five,
she needs good looks. From
thirty-five to fifty-five, good
personality. From fifty-five
on, she needs good cash.

❦ ENTERTAINER SOPHIE TUCKER

The majority of people feel they must be doing something all the time. Many who sit all day in an office or clean the house or work in a factory think that if they sit down at a sidewalk cafe and fold their arms and look at people, they are merely wasting time. They are wrong. In watching people and enjoying life, they may only then be truly alive.

❧ MUSICIAN ARTUR RUBINSTEIN

People tend to gain in tolerance and grow more generous-spirited as they get older, but on the other hand, we often lose connectedness and some degree of interest in what's going on, so our generosity is not all that expensive to us.

❦ WRITER EDWARD HOAGLAND

The once sacred Churches
have fallen into dust and ashes,
yet even now we set our hearts
eagerly upon money. We live as
though we were doomed to die
on the morrow, but we build
houses as though we were going
to live forever in the world.

❦ ST. JEROME

Throughout life, we get clues that remind us of the direction we are supposed to be headed in. If you do not pay attention, then you make lousy choices and end up with a miserable life. If you stay focused, then you learn your lessons and have a full and good life, including a good death.

❦ PSYCHIATRIST ELISABETH KÜBLER-ROSS

Friendship remains.
Somehow, love
remains—and the
most precious gift,
doubt.

❦ WRITER JORGE LUIS BORGES

The whiter my hair becomes, the more ready people are to believe what I say.

❦ PHILOSOPHER BERTRAND RUSSELL

You must learn day by day, year by year, to broaden your horizon. The more things you love, the more you are interested in, the more you enjoy, the more you are indignant about— the more you have left when anything happens.

❦ ACTRESS ETHEL BARRYMORE

You're only as old as you feel is a refrain one hears enough that it must have some truth to it, though your oncologist might disagree.

❧ WRITER EDWARD HOAGLAND

Be an individualist—
and an individual. You'll
be amazed at how much
faster you get ahead.

❦ BUSINESSMAN J. PAUL GETTY

Ever tried. Ever failed.

No matter. Try again.

Fail again. Fail better.

❦ PLAYWRIGHT SAMUEL BECKETT

It is too late! Ah, nothing is too late
Till the tired heart shall cease to palpitate . . .
Chaucer, at Woodstock with the nightingales,
At sixty wrote the Canterbury Tales;
Goethe at Weimar, toiling to the last,
Completed Faust when eighty years were past.
These are indeed exceptions, but they show
How far the gulf-stream of our youth may flow
Into the arctic regions of our lives.

❧ POET HENRY WADSWORTH LONGFELLOW,
"MORITURI SALUTAMUS,"
THE MASQUE OF PANDORA

How unnatural
the imposed view…
that passionate love
belongs only to
the young.

❦ WRITER MAY SARTON

The thing you are ripening toward is the fruit of your life. It will make you bright inside, no matter what you are outside. It is a shining thing.

❦ WRITER STEWART EDWARD WHITE

I cut my own hair.
I got sick of barbers
because they talk too
much. And too much
of their talk was about
my hair falling out.

❦ POET ROBERT FROST

It's ill-becoming for an old broad to sing about how bad she wants it. But occasionally we do.

❦ SINGER LENA HORNE

Time is the substance I am made of. Time is a river which sweeps me along, but I am the river; it is a tiger which destroys me, but I am the tiger; it is a fire which consumes me, but I am the fire. The world, unfortunately, is real; I unfortunately am Borges.

❦ WRITER JORGE LUIS BORGES

Tomorrow I will haul down
   the flag of hypocrisy,
I will devote my grey hairs
   to wine:
My life's span has reached
   seventy,
If I don't enjoy myself now,
   when shall I?

❧ POET OMAR KHAYYÁM,
FROM THE *RUBÁIYÁT*

You have to be at peace with yourself. I love to laugh. I think laughter can cure. You can see it in a person's face. Around age forty, when your face has lost the glow of youth, what you are inside starts to form on the outside. Either the lines go up or they go down. If they go up, that's a good sign.

❦ ACTRESS ELIZABETH TAYLOR

Musicians don't retire;
they stop when there's
no more music in them.

❧ MUSICIAN LOUIS ARMSTRONG

Swim, dance a little,
go to Paris every August,
and live within walking
distance of two hospitals.

❦ HORSE TRAINER HORATIO LURO,
EXPLAINING THE SECRET OF HIS
EIGHTY YEARS

All the clichés say that as you grow older you grow wiser. I don't feel one damn bit wiser! Wisdom is not concomitant with age. I've met some extremely stupid people who as they've hardened and grown older have become more selfish, intolerant, vindictive, driven to outrage easily, and they dwell in their disappointments. But a kind of acceptance isn't easily arrived at. I'm talking about graceful acceptance, a recognition of your own foibles, your own limitations, and I'm not talking of physical limitations. Somehow to make peace with the fact that you, like the trees, plants, and landscapes, are going through an inevitable process.

❦ ACTOR HUME CRONYN

If you have got
a living force and
you're not using it,
nature kicks up
back. The blood
boils just like you
put it in a pot.

❦ ARTIST LOUISE NEVELSON

In youth we learn,
in age we understand.

❧ WRITER MARIE EBNER-ESCHENBACH

When you live with another person for fifty years, all of your memories are invested in that person, like a bank account of shared memories. It's not that you refer to them constantly. In fact, for people who do not live in the past, you almost never say, "Do you remember that night we . . . ?" But you don't have to. That is the best of all. You *know* that the other person *does* remember. Thus, the past is part of the present as long as the other person lives. It is better than any scrapbook, because you are both living scrapbooks.

❦ DIRECTOR FEDERICO FELLINI

The secret to my success was that somehow I always managed to live to fly another day.

❦ TEST PILOT GENERAL CHUCK YEAGER

Courage is a
strange thing:
One can never
be sure of it.

❧ WRITER RAYMOND CHANDLER

Wisdom is learning from all your experience, which means maybe you don't make the same mistakes over and over again. And you're more tolerant. Oh, God, how we need it in the world. Tolerance of other people's religion, aims, points of view. Just to be able to sit still and hear what the person is saying.

❦ ACTRESS JESSICA TANDY

If you have an important point to make, don't try to be subtle or clever. Use a pile driver. Hit the point once. Then come back and hit it again. Then hit it a third time—a tremendous whack.

❦ STATESMAN WINSTON CHURCHILL

Live your life and
forget your age.

❦ PASTOR/WRITER NORMAN VINCENT PEALE

If you want immortality— make it.

❦ POET JOAQUIN MILLER

Well, I'll tell you, young fella, to be truthful and honest and perfectly frank about it, I'm eighty-three years old, which ain't bad. To be truthful and honest and frank about it, the thing I'd like to be right now is an astronaut.

❦ BASEBALL MANAGER CASEY STENGEL

To be seventy years old is like climbing the Alps. You reach a snow-crowned summit, and see behind you the deep valley stretching miles and miles away, and before you other summits higher and whiter, which you may have strength to climb, or may not. Then you sit down and meditate and wonder which it will be.

❦ POET HENRY WADSWORTH LONGFELLOW

Those docs, they always ask you how you live so long. I tell 'em: "If I'd known I was gonna live this long, I'd have taken better care of myself."

❦ MUSICIAN EUBIE BLAKE

The ordinary objects of human endeavor—property, outward success, luxury—have always seemed to me contemptible. I have never looked upon ease and happiness as ends in themselves. Such an ethical basis I call more proper for a herd of swine. The ideals which have lighted me on my way and time after time given me new courage to face life cheerfully have been Truth, Goodness, and Beauty.

❦ PHYSICIST ALBERT EINSTEIN

Everyone has a gift for something, even if it is the gift of being a good friend.

❧ SINGER MARIAN ANDERSON

And here is the prime condition of success, the great secret: Concentrate your energy, thought, and capital exclusively upon the business in which you are engaged. Having begun in one line, resolve to fight it out on that line, to lead in it; adopt every improvement, have the best machinery, and know the most about it.

❦ INDUSTRIALIST ANDREW CARNEGIE

The older you get, the stronger the wind gets— and it's always in your face.

❦ GOLFER JACK NICKLAUS

The old days were the old days. And they were great days. But now is now.

❦ COMEDIAN DON RICKLES

When a man asks himself what is meant by *action,* he proves he isn't a man of action. Action is a lack of balance. In order to act you must be somewhat insane. A reasonably sensible man is satisfied with thinking.

❦ STATESMAN GEORGES CLEMENCEAU

The great thing about getting older is that you don't lose all the other ages you've been.

❦ WRITER MADELEINE L'ENGLE

In the midst of all the doubts which have been discussed for four thousand years in four thousand ways, the safest course is to do nothing against one's conscience. With this secret, we can enjoy life and have no fear of death.

❦ WRITER FRANÇOIS MARIE AROUET DE VOLTAIRE

Every time I think that I'm getting old and gradually going to the grave, something else happens.

☙ MOTHER OF PRESIDENT JIMMY CARTER, LILLIAN CARTER

The fear of death is virtually meaningless. We need to have the humility to know that, in death, we're in the company of countless others, and that death is the only certain destiny that awaits us all. I'm not overly preoccupied with death but rather by the enormous question mark it represents. Is it nothingness? That's possible. If it's not, then what a great adventure lies ahead.

❦ STATESMAN FRANÇOIS MITTERRAND, IN COMMENTS BEFORE HIS DEATH DUE TO PROSTATE CANCER

W hen you get to
my age, life seems
little more than
one long march
to and from the
lavatory.

❧ WRITER JOHN MORTIMER

A woman I graduated from college with told me plastic surgery was vulgar, that lines were a sign of character, that it's beautiful to age. I said bull. Character is internal. If you want to present yourself to the world with a face-lift, why the hell not?

Many women approaching fifty don't feel glamorous; they feel invisible. I think they mean sexually invisible, but if they send out the right vibes, they won't be.

❦ WRITER JUDITH KRANTZ

When one has reached eighty-one, one likes to sit back and let the world turn by itself, without trying to push it.

❦ PLAYWRIGHT SEAN O'CASEY

If you knew that you were going to die tonight, or merely that you would have to go away and never return, would you, looking upon men and things for the last time, see them in the same light that you have hitherto seen them? Would you not love as you never yet have loved?

❦ WRITER MAURICE MAETERLINCK

I am an old man
and have known
many troubles,
but most of them
never happened.

❦ WRITER MARK TWAIN

[H. L. Mencken] told me once that he answered all his mail, pleasant and unpleasant, with just one line: "You may be right." That's the way I feel now. It is in the realm of possibility, just barely, that I could be the one who's wrong.

❦ WRITER CLARE BOOTH LUCE

Our only purpose
in life is growth.
There are no
accidents.

❦ PSYCHIATRIST ELISABETH KÜBLER-ROSS

He who is of a calm
and happy nature will
hardly feel the pressure
of age, but to him
who is of an opposite
disposition, youth
and age are equally
a burden.

❦ PHILOSOPHER PLATO

Choose well:
Your choice is
brief and yet
endless.

❦ WRITER ELLA WINTER

I get up before anyone
else in my household,
not because sleep has
deserted me in my
advancing years, but
because an intense
eagerness to live draws
me from my bed.

❦ WRITER MAURICE GOUDEKET

However often the thread may be torn out of your hands, you must develop enough patience to wind it up again and again.

❦ ARCHITECT WALTER GROPIUS

Age only matters when one is aging. Now that I have arrived at a great age, I might just as well be twenty.

❧ ARTIST PABLO PICASSO

Now, supposing the caterpillars have an annual meeting, the local society of caterpillars. . . . And . . . an older caterpillar says, "You know, it's an extraordinary thing, but we are all going to be butterflies." "Okay," the caterpillars say, "you poor fool, you are just an old man who is frightened of dying; you're inventing something to comfort yourself." But these are all the things that people say to me when I say I am looking forward to dying because I know that I am going to go into eternity. You see?

❦ JOURNALIST MALCOLM MUGGERIDGE

After age seventy it's patch, patch, patch.

❦ ACTOR JIMMY STEWART

During much of my life, I was anxious to be what someone else wanted me to be. Now I have given up that struggle. I am what I am.

❦ POET ELIZABETH COATSWORTH

One of the things that happens when you get older is your ear hairs really start growing. Can't stand 'em, so I wax 'em out. Barber pours the wax around my ears, lets it settle, then pulls. You can hear a ripping noise as the hairs come out.

❦ FINANCIER T. BOONE PICKENS

One starts to get young at the age of sixty, and then it is too late.

❦ ARTIST PABLO PICASSO

One must wager on the future. To save the life of a single child, no effort is superfluous. To make a tired old man smile is to perform an essential task. To defeat injustice and misfortune, if only for one instant, for a single victim, is to invent a new reason to hope.

❦ WRITER ELIE WIESEL

I am delighted to find that even at my age great ideas come to me, the pursuit and development of which should require another lifetime.

❦ WRITER JOHANN WOLFGANG VON GOETHE

What a strange thing is memory, and hope; one looks backward, the other forward. The one is of today, the other is the tomorrow. Memory is history recorded in our brain, memory is a painter; it paints pictures of the past and of the day.

❧ ARTIST GRANDMA MOSES

Never feel self-pity, the most destructive emotion there is. How awful to be caught up in the terrible squirrel cage of self.

❦ POLITICIAN MILLICENT FENWICK

A man is not old as long as he is seeking something.

❦ BIOLOGIST/WRITER JEAN ROSTAND

What remains to me of strength becomes more precious for what is lost. I have lost one ear, but was never so alive to sweet sounds as now. My sight is so far impaired that the brightness in which nature was revealed to me in my youth is dimmed, but I never looked on nature with such pure joy as now. My limbs soon tire, but I never felt it such a privilege to move about in the open air, under the sky in sight of the infinity of creation, as at this moment. I almost think that my simple food, eaten by rule, was never relished so well. I am grateful, then, for my earthly tabernacle, though it does creak and shake not a little.

❦ CLERGYMAN WILLIAM ELLERY CHANNING

Life has got to
be lived—that's
all there is to it.

❦ HUMANITARIAN ELEANOR ROOSEVELT

For the first time, I have lately become aware of the fact that the period of our earthly existence is limited. During the whole of my life, this idea has never actually come into my mind. It occurred to me very distinctly when I was looking at an old tree there in the garden. When we came, it was very small, and I looked at it from above. Now, it waves high above my head and seems to say, "You will soon depart, but I shall stay here for hundreds more years."

❦ COMPOSER JEAN SIBELIUS

There's that "You're only as old as you feel" business, which is fine to a point, but you can't be Shirley Temple on the Good Ship Lollipop forever. Sooner or later, dammit, you're *old*.

❦ ACTRESS JOAN CRAWFORD

I am profoundly grateful to old age, which has increased my eagerness for conversation and taken away that for food and drink.

❧ ORATOR/STATESMAN CICERO (MARCUS TULLIUS CICERO)

As an old man, looking back on one's life, it's one of the things that strikes you most forcibly—that the only thing that's taught one anything is *suffering*. Not success, not happiness, not anything like that. The only thing that *really* teaches one what life's about— the joy of understanding, the joy of coming in contact with what life *really* signifies—is suffering, affliction.

❧ JOURNALIST MALCOLM MUGGERIDGE

Whenever a man's friends begin to compliment him about looking young, he may be sure they think he is getting old.

❦ WRITER WASHINGTON IRVING

Age seldom arrives smoothly or quickly. It's more often a succession of jerks.

❦ WRITER JEAN RHYS

One of the greatest handicaps is to fear a mistake. You have stopped yourself. You have to move freely into the arena, not just to wait for the perfect situation, the perfect moment. . . . If you have to make a mistake, it's better to make a mistake of action than one of inaction. If I had the opportunity again, I would take chances.

❦ DIRECTOR FEDERICO FELLINI

They say stress is a killer. But I think *no* stress is equally deadly, especially as you get older. If your days just seem to slip by without any highs and lows, without some anxieties and pulse-quickening occurrences, you may not be *really living*.

❦ ACTRESS HELEN HAYES

I'm just the same age I've always been.

❦ WRITER CAROLYN WELLS

It is really something of a feat to have lived seventy-five years, in spite of illnesses, germs, accidents, disasters, and wars. And now every fresh day finds me more filled with wonder and better qualified to draw the last drop of delight from it.

❦ WRITER MAURICE GOUDEKET

People always ask me what death is like. I tell them it is glorious. It is the easiest thing they will ever do.

Life is hard. Life is a struggle.

Life is like going to school. You are given many lessons. The more you learn, the harder the lessons become.

❦ PSYCHIATRIST ELISABETH KÜBLER-ROSS

Every day in my old age is more important than I can say. It will never return. When one takes one's leave of life, one notices how much one has left undone.

❦ COMPOSER JEAN SIBELIUS

In July, when I bury my nose in a hazel bush, I feel fifteen years old again. It's good! It smells of love!

❦ ARTIST CAMILLE COROT

A life directed chiefly toward the fulfillment of personal desires will sooner or later always lead to bitterness.

❦ PHYSICIST ALBERT EINSTEIN

It is the beginning of the end when you discover you have style.

❦ WRITER DASHIELL HAMMETT

I am perhaps the oldest
musician in the world.
I am an old man but
in many senses a very
young man. And this is
what I want you to be,
young, young all your
life, and to say things to
the world that are true.

❦ MUSICIAN PABLO CASALS

The closing years
of life are like
the end of a
masquerade party,
when the masks
are dropped.

❦ PHILOSOPHER ARTHUR SCHOPENHAUER

Last night I had a typical cholesterol-free dinner: baked squash, skimmed milk, and gelatin. I'm sure this will not make me live any longer, but I know it's going to seem longer.

❦ COMEDIAN GROUCHO MARX

One can savor sights and sounds more deeply when one gets really old. It may be the last time you see a sunset, a tree, the snow, or know winter. The sea, a lake, all become as in childhood, magical and a great wonder: then seen for the first time, now perhaps for the last. Music, bird songs, the wind, the waves: One listens to tones with deeper delight and appreciation— "loving well," to borrow from Shakespeare's seventy-third sonnet, "that which I must leave ere long."

❦ WRITER HELEN NEARING

My experience has been in a short seventy-seven years . . . that in the end when you fight for a desperate cause and have good reasons to fight, you usually win.

❦ PHYSICIST EDWARD TELLER

Winter is on my head, but eternal spring is in my heart. The nearer I approach the end, the plainer I hear around me the immortal symphonies of the worlds which invite me. . . . For half a century I have been writing thoughts in prose, verse, history, drama, romance, tradition, satire, ode, and song. I have tried them all, but I feel I have not said a thousandth part of that which is within me. When I go down to the grave, I can say, "I have finished my day's work," but I cannot say, "I have finished my life's work."

❦ WRITER VICTOR HUGO

I'm incredibly lucky to still be around, doing all the things I want to do and getting extremely well paid for it. There's a parallel with golf—a lot of it is in the mind, and the moment you start to lose the enthusiasm or appetite, it affects your judgements and decisions. And then you stop performing well. I think enthusiasm and appetite are more important than anything.

❦ ACTOR SEAN CONNERY

The young man who has not wept is a savage, and the old man who will not laugh is a fool.

❦ WRITER GEORGE SANTAYANA

Life is moments, day by day, not
a chronometer or a contractual
commitment by God. The digits
of one's age do not correspond to
the arrhythmia of one's heart or
to the secret chemistry in our lymph
nodes that, mysteriously going rancid,
can betray us despite all the surgery,
dentistry, and other codger-friendly
amenities that money buys. Nor
do good works keep you off the
undertaker's slab. But cheeriness,
maybe yes. Cheery, lean little guys
do seem to squeeze an extra decade
out of the miser above. . . .

❦ WRITER EDWARD HOAGLAND

The greatest dignity
to be found in death
is the dignity of the
life that preceded it.
Hope resides in the
meaning of what
our lives have been.

❦ SURGEON SHERWIN B. NULAND

It reduces itself to this. You have to be in the right place at the right time, but when it comes, you better have something on the ball.

❦ COMEDIAN GROUCHO MARX

Age puzzles me.
I thought it was a
quiet time. My seventies
were interesting and
fairly serene, but my
eighties are passionate.
I grow more intense
as I age.

❦ WRITER FLORIDA SCOTT-MAXWELL

REPORTER: "What do you expect the future to be like?"

VERY OLD WOMAN: "Very short."

❦ ONE OF THE OLDEST WOMEN IN FRANCE, SPOKEN DURING A BIRTHDAY INTERVIEW

It's taken me all
my life to learn
what not to play.

❦ MUSICIAN DIZZY GILLESPIE

I have had dreams and I've had nightmares. I overcame the nightmares because of my dreams.

❦ VIROLOGIST JONAS SALK

I have learned to
read the papers
calmly and not
to hate the fools
I read about.

❦ CRITIC EDMUND WILSON

We need to find God, and he can't be found in noise and restlessness. God is the friend of silence. See how nature—trees, flowers, grass—grows in silence; see the stars, the moon, and the sun, see how they move in silence. We need silence to be able to touch souls.

❧ HUMANITARIAN MOTHER TERESA

After your death,
you will be what
you were before
your birth.

❦ PHILOSOPHER ARTHUR SCHOPENHAUER

A long life makes me feel nearer truth, yet it won't go into words, so how can I convey it? I can't, and I want to. I want to tell people approaching and perhaps fearing age that it is a time of discovery. If they say—"Of what?" I can only answer, "We must find out for ourselves, otherwise it won't be discovery." I want to say— "If at the end of your life you have only yourself, it is much. Look, you will find."

❧ WRITER FLORIDA SCOTT-MAXWELL

However toplofty and idealistic a man may be, he can always rationalize his right to earn money.

❦ WRITER RAYMOND CHANDLER

If I had my life
to live over again,
I'd make the same
mistakes—only
sooner.

❦ ACTRESS TALLULAH BANKHEAD

I have seen and believe in goodness, the indefinable quality which is immediately and unhesitatingly recognized by the most different kinds of men: the simple goodness of an old nurse or the mother of a large family; the more complex and costly goodness of a priest, a doctor, or a teacher.

❦ WRITER IRIS ORIGO

At seventy, I would say the advantage is that you take life more calmly. You have that "this, too, shall pass!"

❦ HUMANITARIAN ELEANOR ROOSEVELT

Go ahead and do it. It's much easier to apologize after something's been done than to get permission ahead of time.

❦ MATHEMATICIAN GRACE MURRAY HOPPER

Tomorrow I shall be sixty-nine, but I do not seem to care. I did not start the affair, and I have not been consulted about it at any step.

❦ WRITER WILLIAM DEAN HOWELLS, IN A LETTER TO MARK TWAIN

Once upon a time, Chuang Chou dreamt that he was a butterfly, fluttering happily like a butterfly. He was conscious only of his happiness as a butterfly, unaware that he was Chuang Chou. Suddenly he awakened, and there he was, veritably Chuang Chou himself. Now he does not know whether the butterfly is a dream of Chuang Chou or whether Chuang Chou is a dream of the butterfly.

❦ PHILOSOPHER CHUANG-TZU

Life itself is the proper binge.

❦ CHEF JULIA CHILD

When I was young,
I used to have successes
with women because
I was young. Now I
have successes with
women because I am
old. Middle age was
the hard part.

🍎 MUSICIAN ARTUR RUBINSTEIN

Oh, death is no problem for me. If I go while we're talking, I'm ready. My mother had a wonderful philosophy on that. Every time she lost somebody, it was, "Well, there's one thing we don't know the answer to—and now he knows it."

❦ ACTRESS BETTY WHITE

Lifelong enemies are, I think, as hard to make and as important to one's well-being as friends.

🐛 WRITER JESSICA MITFORD

When I was young,
I observed that nine
out of every ten
things I did were
failures, so I did ten
times more work.

❦ WRITER GEORGE BERNARD SHAW

As I age, I notice my body doing something, and I want to see what it's doing. I don't want to interfere with that. It knows something I don't. It's like being pregnant. You don't know how to age, except intellectually. But your body knows. I think I first noticed this when I thought about menopause because I saw that my body was getting rid of everything it needed to produce another person and retaining that which was necessary to support one person. It was a process I was observing, not directing. It gives you some respect for the wisdom of the body.

❦ FEMINIST GLORIA STEINEM

I regret having
been so polite in
the past. I'd like to
trample on at least
a dozen people.

❦ WRITER HAROLD BRODKEY

I don't know whether my life has been a success or a failure. But not having any anxiety about becoming one instead of the other, and just taking things as they came along, I've had a lot of extra time to enjoy life.

❦ COMEDIAN HARPO MARX

Our greatest glory
is not in never falling
but in rising every
time we fall.

❦ PHILOSOPHER CONFUCIUS

 B ut what signifies our wishing?
Things happen, after all, as they will
happen. I have sung that wishing song
a thousand times when I was young,
and now find, at fourscore, that the
three contraries have befallen me, being
subject to the gout and the stone, and
being not yet master of all my passions—
like the proud girl in my country who
wished and resolved not to marry
a parson, nor a Presbyterian, nor an
Irishman, and at length found herself
married to an Irish Presbyterian parson.

❦ STATESMAN BENJAMIN FRANKLIN

My idea of forgiveness is letting go of resentment that does not serve your better interest, ridding yourself of negative thoughts. All they do is make you miserable. Believe me, you can fret and fume all you want, but whoever it was that wronged you is not suffering from your anguish whatsoever.

❦ ACTRESS DELLA REESE

You can't reach old age by another man's road. My habits protect my life but they would assassinate you.

❦ WRITER MARK TWAIN,
FROM HIS SEVENTIETH-BIRTHDAY SPEECH

When I was forty and looking at sixty, it seemed like a thousand miles away. But sixty-two feels like a week and a half away from eighty. I must now get on with those things I always talked about doing but put off.

❦ ACTOR/SINGER HARRY BELAFONTE

Perhaps the most
important things
are those we don't
remember in
a precise way,
that we remember
unconsciously.

❦ WRITER JORGE LUIS BORGES

Beyond the age of eighty, the perspectives of a lifetime wither and shrink like all else. You feel that your mortal car is straddling the median line and the right-hand wheels are rumbling in this world with the other two in the other one.

❧ WRITER SAUL BELLOW

The longer I live,
the more beautiful
life becomes.

❧ ARCHITECT FRANK LLOYD WRIGHT

When I was young,
I was amazed at Plutarch's
statement that the elder Cato
began at the age of eighty to
learn Greek. I am amazed no
longer. Old age is ready to
undertake tasks that youth
shirked because they would
take too long.

❦ WRITER W. SOMERSET MAUGHAM

When grace combines with wrinkles, it is admirable. There is an indescribable light of dawn about intensely happy old age. . . . The young man is handsome, but the old, superb.

❦ WRITER VICTOR HUGO

Young man, the secret of my success is that at an early age I discovered I was not God.

❦ JURIST OLIVER WENDELL HOLMES JR.

Growing old— it's not nice, but it's interesting.

❦ PLAYWRIGHT AUGUST STRINDBERG

When we recall the past, we usually find that it is the simplest things—not the great occasions—that in retrospect give off the greatest glory of happiness.

❧ COMEDIAN BOB HOPE

One thing I have certainly learnt— not to have a good opinion of myself.

❦ THEOLOGIAN WILLIAM RALPH INGE

I don't think anyone "bounces back"—that sounds so easy—but you can work through it. I don't want to sound corny, but I've prayed a lot. I could have been destroyed if I hadn't been religious and strong. Sure, I've had some tough breaks, but I tell myself, "I ain't down yet!"

❦ ACTRESS DEBBIE REYNOLDS

To me, old age is always fifteen years older than I am.

❦ FINANCIER BERNARD BARUCH

Social pressure is the enemy! I've seen it happen. How in heaven's name are you going to find your own track if you are always doing what society tells you to do? I also spent a year teaching in a busy prep school, and that was a crowd that was trying to make up their minds, you know? I've seen them since, and those who followed their zeal, their bliss, they have led decent, wonderful lives; those that did what Dad said they should do because it's safe found out it's not safe. It's disaster.

❦ SCHOLAR JOSEPH CAMPBELL

I adore life but I don't fear death. I just prefer to die as late as possible.

❦ WRITER GEORGES SIMENON

Like our shadows
Our wishes lengthen
as the sun declines.

❦ POET EDWARD YOUNG

A man ninety years old was asked to what he attributed his longevity. "I reckon," he said, with a twinkle in his eye, "it's because most nights I went to bed and slept when I should have sat up and worried."

❦ WRITER DOROTHEA KENT

To every man
is given the key
to the gates of
heaven; the same
key opens the
gates of hell.

❦ PHYSICIST RICHARD P. FEYNMAN

The average man generally feels once in his life the full happiness of love and once the joy of freedom. Once in his life he hates bitterly. Once with deep grief he buries a loved one, and once, finally, he dies himself. That is too little for our innate capacity to love, hate, enjoy, and suffer. We exercise daily to strengthen our muscles and sinews that they may not degenerate. But our spiritual organs, which were created for a lifetime of full activity, remain unused, undeveloped, and so, with the passing years, they lose their productive power.

❧ ACTOR EDWARD G. ROBINSON

If you think you
can, you can. And
if you think you
can't, you're right.

❧ BUSINESS EXECUTIVE MARY KAY ASH

Most people are such fools that it is really no great compliment to say that a man is above the average.

❦ WRITER W. SOMERSET MAUGHAM

In the last analysis, getting old is an aspect of the transitoriness of human existence. But this transitoriness can be a strong motivation for our responsibilities—our recognition of responsibility as basic to human existence. It may be proper to repeat the logotherapeutic maxim as I formulated it in a dream. . . . "Live as if you were already living for a second time and as if you had made the mistakes you are about to make now." And indeed, one's sense of responsibility can be heightened by such a fictive autobiographical view of one's own life.

❦ PHYSICIAN/PSYCHOTHERAPIST
VICTOR FRANKL, FROM HIS LAST BOOK,
WRITTEN AT NINETY

Try to keep your soul young and quivering right up to old age, and to imagine right up to the brink of death that life is only beginning. I think that is the only way to keep adding to one's talent, to one's affections, and to one's inner happiness.

❦ WRITER GEORGE SAND

Once in Eugene, Oregon, after a lecture in which I had dealt with the age stages as described by Dante, this young woman comes up to me and says, "Well, Dr. Campbell, you don't understand. Today we go directly from infancy to wisdom." I said, "That's marvelous. All you've missed is life."

❦ SCHOLAR JOSEPH CAMPBELL

In a curious way,
age is simpler than
youth, for it has
so many fewer
options.

❦ POET STANLEY KUNITZ

The tragedy of life is not in the fact of death. The tragedy of life is in what dies inside a man while he lives—the death of genuine feeling, the death of inspired response; the death of awareness that makes it possible to feel the pain or the glory of other men in oneself. . . . No man need fear death: He need fear only that he may die without having known his greatest power—the power of his free will to give his life for others.

❦ MISSIONARY AND PHILOSOPHER
ALBERT SCHWEITZER

Success is a two-bladed golden sword; it knights one and stabs one at the same time.

❦ ACTRESS MAE WEST

Don't ever underestimate
the importance of money.
I know it's often been said
that money won't make you
happy, and this is undeniably
true, but everything else
being equal, it's a lovely thing
to have around the house.

❦ COMEDIAN GROUCHO MARX

The woman who has a gift for old age is the woman who delights in comfort. If warmth is known as the blessing it is, if your bed, your bath, your best-liked food and drink are regarded as fresh delights, then you know how to thrive when old.

❧ WRITER FLORIDA SCOTT-MAXWELL

It is better to be
approximately right
than precisely wrong.

❦ FINANCIER WARREN BUFFETT

I do not believe that true optimism can come about except through tragedy.

❦ WRITER MADELEINE L'ENGLE

Age is nothing
but experience,
and some of us are
more experienced
than others.

❦ HUMORIST ANDY ROONEY

I asked myself the question "What do you want of your life?" and I realized with a start of recognition and terror "Exactly what I have —but to be commensurate, to handle it all better."

❦ WRITER MAY SARTON

If we do not
know about life,
how can we know
about death?

❦ PHILOSOPHER CONFUCIUS

Old age is like climbing a mountain. You climb from ledge to ledge. The higher you get, the more tired and breathless you become, but your views become more extensive.

❦ ACTRESS INGRID BERGMAN

On the whole, age comes
more gently to those who
have some doorway into
an abstract world—art or
philosophy or learning—
regions where the years are
scarcely noticed and the
young and the old can meet
in a pale, truthful light.

❦ WRITER FREYA STARK

You can't have everything, even in California.

❦ WRITER RAYMOND CHANDLER

There is a certain kind of carefree that returns to you in old age, different from the carefree of youth when you didn't know any better. It's more like being free of caring. It isn't joyous at all, as it was in youth, but it is a kind of freedom, and all kinds of freedom are precious in some way.

❧ DIRECTOR FEDERICO FELLINI

Obey the voice within—
it commands us to give of
ourselves and help others.
As long as we have the
capacity to give, we are alive.

❦ ACTOR KIRK DOUGLAS

To be astonished
is one of the surest
ways of not growing
old too quickly.

❦ WRITER COLETTE

Don't complain about old age. How much good it has brought me that was unexpected and beautiful. I concluded from that that the end of old age and life will be just as unexpectedly beautiful. . . .

❧ WRITER LEO TOLSTOY

No matter how
old a mother is,
she watches her
middle-aged
children for signs
of improvement.

❦ WRITER FLORIDA SCOTT-MAXWELL

I've always been in the right place at the right time. Of course, I steered myself there.

❦ COMEDIAN BOB HOPE

To enter the country of old age is a new experience, different from what you supposed it to be. Nobody, man or woman, knows the country until he has lived in it and has taken out his citizenship papers.

❦ CRITIC AND EDITOR MALCOLM COWLEY

If I had my life to live over again,
I would have made a rule to read
some poetry and listen to some
music at least once a week; for
perhaps the parts of my brain now
atrophied would thus have been
kept active through use. The loss
of these tastes is a loss of happiness,
and may possibly be injurious
to the intellect, and more probably
the moral character, by enfeebling
the emotional part of our nature.

❧ NATURALIST CHARLES DARWIN

That's the difference between a champ and a knife thrower. The champ may have lost his stuff temporarily or permanently, he can't be sure. But when he can no longer throw his hard high one, he throws his heart instead. He throws something. He just doesn't walk off the mound and weep.

❦ WRITER RAYMOND CHANDLER

I am aware that life was never
perfect, never absolute. This bestows
contentment, even a fearlessness.
Separation, detachment, death.
I look upon another's insistence
on the merits of his or her life,
duties, intellect, accomplishment,
and see that most of it is nonsense.
And me, hell, I am a genius or
I am a fraud . . .

❦ WRITER HAROLD BRODKEY

Sometimes I wonder whether I've given up too much for the theatre, but I have one big consolation—money.

❦ ACTRESS HERMIONE GINGOLD

The real challenge is not simply to survive. Hell, anyone can do that. It's to survive as yourself, undiminished.

❦ DIRECTOR ELIA KAZAN

Discussing how old you are is the temple of boredom.

❦ ACTRESS/WRITER RUTH GORDON

Life is the combination
of magic and pasta,
of fantasy and of reality.

❦ DIRECTOR FEDERICO FELLINI

[At my age] getting a second doctor's opinion is kind of like switching slot machines.

☙ STATESMAN JIMMY CARTER

Old age hangs on you like an old overcoat.

❦ WRITER QUENTIN CRISP

The years seem to rush by now, and I think of death as a fast-approaching end of a journey. Double and treble reason for loving as well as working while it is day.

❦ WRITER GEORGE ELIOT, IN THE LAST YEAR OF HER LIFE

Hell begins on the day when God grants us a clear vision of all that we might have achieved, of all the gifts which we have wasted, of all that we might have done which we did not do. . . . For me the conception of Hell lies in two words: "too late."

❦ COMPOSER GIAN-CARLO MENOTTI

At twenty, a man is full of fight and hope. He wants to reform the world. When he is seventy, he still wants to reform the world, but he knows he can't.

❦ LAWYER CLARENCE DARROW

Celebrate your success and find humor in your failures. Don't take yourself so seriously. Loosen up and everyone around you will loosen up. Have fun and always show enthusiasm. When all else fails put on a costume and sing a silly song.

❦ BUSINESS EXECUTIVE SAM WALTON

The story of a love
is not important—
what is important is
that one is capable of
love. It's perhaps the
only glimpse we are
permitted of eternity.

❦ ACTRESS HELEN HAYES

When you know
you're right, you don't
care what others think.
You know sooner or
later it will come out
in the wash.

❦ GENETICIST/BOTANIST
BARBARA McCLINTOCK

Why endeavor to straighten the road of life? The faster we travel, the less there is to see.

❦ ACTRESS HELEN HAYES

When you are younger, you get blamed for crimes you never committed, and when you're older, you begin to get credit for virtues you never possessed. It evens itself out.

❧ WRITER I. F. STONE

I live now on borrowed time, waiting in the anteroom for the summons that will inevitably come. And then—I go on to the next thing, whatever it is. One luckily doesn't have to bother about that.

❦ WRITER AGATHA CHRISTIE

Old age equalizes—
we are unaware that
what is happening to
us has happened to
untold numbers from
the beginning of time.
When we are young,
we act as if we were
the first young people
in the world.

❦ WRITER/PHILOSOPHER ERIC HOFFER

I'm going to be eighty soon, and I guess the one thing that puzzles me most is how quick it got here.

❧ MUSICIAN ROY ACUFF

Old age is like
everything else.
To make a success
of it, you've got
to start young.

❦ ACTOR FRED ASTAIRE

Let us cherish and love old age; for it is full of pleasure, if you know how to use it. The best morsel is reserved for last.

❦ PHILOSOPHER/WRITER SENECA (LUCIUS ANNAEUS SENECA)

When young,
beware of fighting;
when strong, beware
of sex; and when old,
beware of possession.

❦ PHILOSOPHER CONFUCIUS

I hope I have a young outlook. Since I have an old everything else, this is my one chance of having a bit of youth as a part of me.

❦ WRITER RICHARD ARMOUR

Living is strife and torment, disappointment and love and sacrifice, golden sunsets and black storms. I said that some time ago, and today I do not think I would add one word.

❦ ACTOR LAURENCE OLIVIER

Don't grow old
without money,
honey.

❦ SINGER LENA HORNE

Money is boring. When you get to my age, you don't know what to spend it on. When I was your age, I was "money, money, money" . . . "save, save." Now, what does it matter?

❦ DIRECTOR BILLY WILDER

From my experience of life I believe my personal motto should be "Beware of men bearing flowers."

❦ WRITER MURIEL SPARK

Give me all the
luxuries of life,
and I will willingly
do without the
necessities.

❦ COMMENT OFTEN MADE BY
FRANK LLOYD WRIGHT—AND
QUOTED IN HIS OBITUARY

White we drink, and call
for garlands, for perfumes
and for maidens,
Old age is creeping on us
unperceived.

❦ SATIRIST JUVENAL
(DECIMUS JUNIUS JUVENALIS)

The only sin is mediocrity.

❦ DANCER AND CHOREOGRAPHER
MARTHA GRAHAM

Life has taught
me that it is not
for our faults that
we are disliked and
even hated, but for
our qualities.

❦ CRITIC BERNARD BERENSON

The great secret that all
old people share is that
you really haven't changed
in seventy or eighty years.
Your body changes, but
you don't change at all.
And that, of course,
causes great confusion.

❦ WRITER DORIS LESSING

Twenty can't be expected to tolerate sixty in all things, and sixty gets bored stiff with twenty's eternal love affairs.

❦ WRITER EMILY CARR

Old age is an excellent time for outrage. My goal is to say or do at least one outrageous thing every week.

❦ ACTIVIST MAGGIE KUHN

Sixty years ago, I knew everything; now I know nothing; education is a progressive discovery of our own ignorance.

❦ HISTORIAN WILL DURANT

It is one of the mysteries of our nature that a man, all unprepared, can take a thunderbolt like that and live. There is but one reasonable explanation of it. The intellect is stunned by the shock and but gropingly gathers the meaning of the words. The power to realize their full import is mercifully lacking. It will take mind and memory months and possibly years to gather together the details and thus learn and know the whole extent of the loss.

❦ WRITER MARK TWAIN,
WRITING ABOUT THE DEATH OF
HIS DAUGHTER DUE TO MENINGITIS

It's life, isn't it? You plow ahead and make a hit. And you plow on and someone passes you. Then someone passes them. Time levels.

❦ ACTRESS KATHARINE HEPBURN

Inside every seventy-year-old is a thirty-five-year-old asking, "What happened?"

❦ ADVICE-COLUMNIST ANN LANDERS

My rule of life prescribed as an absolutely sacred rite smoking cigars and also the drinking of alcohol before, after, and, if need be, during all meals and in the intervals between them.

❦ STATESMAN WINSTON CHURCHILL

I, personally, have succeeded in living nearly eighty–five years without taking any trouble about my diet.

❦ PHILOSOPHER BERTRAND RUSSELL

During my long life, I have learned one lesson: that the most important thing is to realize why one is alive— and I think it is not only to build bridges or tall buildings or make money, but to do something truly important, to do something for humanity. To bring joy, hope, to make life richer for the spirit because you have been alive, that is the most important thing.

❧ MUSICIAN ARTUR RUBINSTEIN

I am old enough
to tell the truth.
It is one of the
privileges of age.

❦ STATESMAN GEORGES CLEMENCEAU

Do not grow old,
no matter how long
you live. Never cease
to stand like curious
children before the
Great Mystery into
which we were born.

☙ PHYSICIST ALBERT EINSTEIN

Luck is a dividend of sweat. The more you sweat, the luckier you get.

❦ BUSINESS EXECUTIVE RAY KROC

When I was young,
there was no respect
for the young, and now
that I am old, there is
no respect for the old.
I missed out coming
and going.

❦ WRITER J. B. PRIESTLEY

[Humor] keeps [the elderly] rolling
along, singing a song. When you laugh,
it's an involuntary explosion of the lungs.
The lungs need to replenish themselves
with oxygen. So you laugh, you breathe,
the blood runs, and everything is
circulating. If you don't laugh, you'll die.

❧ DIRECTOR/WRITER MEL BROOKS

It may be necessary temporarily to accept a lesser evil, but one must never label a necessary evil as good.

❦ ANTHROPOLOGIST MARGARET MEAD

The best way to adjust—no, ignore—most of the negative thoughts about aging is to say to yourself, with conviction, "I am still the *very same* person I have been all of my adult life." You *are,* you know.

❦ ACTRESS HELEN HAYES

Any life, no matter how long and complex it may be, is made up of a *single moment*— the moment in which a man finds out, once and for all, who he is.

❦ WRITER JORGE LUIS BORGES

When I was young,
I found out that the
big toe always ends up
making a hole in a sock.
So I stopped wearing
socks.

❧ PHYSICIST ALBERT EINSTEIN

If you've never been
hated by your child,
you've never been
a parent.

❦ ACTRESS BETTE DAVIS

Old age is like a plane flying through a storm. Once you are aboard, there is nothing you can do.

❦ POLITICIAN GOLDA MEIR

Friend, you are a divine mingle-mangle of guts and stardust. So hang in there! If doors opened for me, they can open for anyone.

❦ DIRECTOR FRANK CAPRA

It is in the nature of all things that take form to dissolve again. Strive with your whole being to attain perfection.

❧ BUDDHA, AT HIS DEATH

Avoid fried meats which angry up the blood. If your stomach disputes you, lie down and pacify it with cool thoughts. Keep the juices flowing by jangling around gently as you move. Go very light on vices, such as carrying on in society. The social ramble ain't restful. Avoid running at all times. Don't look back. Something may be gaining on you.

❦ BASEBALL STAR SATCHEL PAIGE

I like living. I have sometimes been wildly, despairingly, acutely miserable, racked with sorrow, but through it all, I still know quite certainly that just to be alive is a grand thing.

❦ WRITER AGATHA CHRISTIE

If I had known when I was twenty-one that I should be as happy as I am now, I should have been sincerely shocked. They promised me wormwood and the funeral raven.

❦ WRITER CHRISTOPHER ISHERWOOD

We're all of us a little greedy.
(Some of us are *plenty* greedy.)
We're all somewhat courageous,
and we're all considerably
cowardly. We're all imperfect,
and life is simply a perpetual,
unending struggle against those
imperfections.

❦ ACTOR SIDNEY POITIER

To be seventy years young is sometimes far more cheerful and hopeful than to be forty years old.

❦ POET/PHYSICIAN
OLIVER WENDELL HOLMES SR.

. . . I look upon death
to be as necessary to our
constitution as sleep.
We shall rise refreshed
in the morning.

❦ STATESMAN BENJAMIN FRANKLIN

There was never a great character who did not sometimes smash the routine regulations and make new ones for himself.

❧ INDUSTRIALIST ANDREW CARNEGIE

I am eighty years old.
There seems to be nothing
to add to this statement.
I have reached the age of
undecorated facts—facts
that refuse to be softened
by sentiment or confused
by nobility of phrase.

❦ WRITER AGNES REPPLIER

I've never really
learnt how to live,
and I've discovered
too late that life is
for living.

❦ BUSINESS EXECUTIVE/POLITICIAN
JOHN CHARLES WALSHAM REITH

A schoolmaster of mine long ago said: You can only learn from the second-raters. The first-raters are out of range; you can't see how they get their effects.

❦ WRITER RAYMOND CHANDLER

If He has given us one marvelous gift, it is that He does not permit us to know the future. It would be unbearable.

❦ ACTOR EDWARD G. ROBINSON

The average man,
who does not know
what to do with
his life, wants
another which
will last forever.

❦ WRITER ANATOLE FRANCE

My eyes have seen much,
but they are not weary.
My ears have heard much,
but they thirst for more.

❦ WRITER RABINDRANATH TAGORE

Hold fast to time! Use it! Be conscious of each day, each hour! They slip away unnoticed all too easily and swiftly.

❦ WRITER THOMAS MANN

During my eighty-seven years, I have witnessed a whole succession of technological revolutions; but none of them has done away with the need for character in the individual, or the ability to think.

❦ FINANCIER BERNARD BARUCH

What I hate most in life are people who are not really the peach of the day but who want to be young and sexy. You can fool nobody. There is a moment when you have to accept that somebody else is younger and fresher and hotter. Life is not a beauty contest.

❦ FASHION DESIGNER KARL LAGERFELD

No endeavor that is worthwhile is simple in prospect; if it is right, it will be simple in retrospect.

❦ PHYSICIST EDWARD TELLER

How old would you be if you didn't know how old you was?

❦ BASEBALL STAR SATCHEL PAIGE

The great man is
one who never loses
his child's heart.

❦ PHILOSOPHER MENCIUS

I want to die young at an advanced age.

❦ JOURNALIST MAX LERNER

Keep looking tanned,
live in an elegant building
(even if you're in the cellar),
be seen in smart restaurants
(even if you nurse one
drink), and if you borrow,
borrow big.

❧ BUSINESSMAN ARISTOTLE ONASSIS

You end up as you deserve. In old age you must put up with the face, the friends, the health, and the children you have earned.

❦ WRITER FAY WELDON

If I would be a young man
again and had to decide how
to make my living, I would
not try to become a scientist
or teacher. I would rather
choose to be a plumber or
a peddler in the hope to
find that modest degree of
independence still available
under present circumstances.

❦ PHYSICIST ALBERT EINSTEIN

Unfortunately, many
people do not consider
fun an important item
on their daily agenda.
For me, that was always
high priority in whatever
I was doing.

❦ TEST PILOT GENERAL CHUCK YEAGER

When [my mother] was dying,
talking to me, she said: "Always try
and be kind and nice to people.
And if you do that, somebody
will always speak up for you."
And I've found that to be a fact.
They really do.

❦ MUSICIAN **B.B. KING**

I have found the best way to give advice to your children is to find out what they want and then advise them to do it.

❦ STATESMAN HARRY S TRUMAN

Don't believe all the baloney people tell you when they're describing what they're going to do for you someday soon. *Nem di gelt* [Get the money].

❦ COMEDIAN HENNY YOUNGMAN

The future? Like unwritten books and unborn children, you don't talk about it.

❦ SINGER DIETRICH FISCHER-DIESKAU

1. Never lose interest in life and the world.

2. Eat sparingly and at regular hours.

3. Take plenty of exercise but not too much.

4. Get plenty of sleep.

5. Never allow yourself to become annoyed.

6. Set a daily schedule of life and keep it.

7. Get a lot of sunlight.

8. Drink as much milk as will agree with you.

9. Obey your doctor and consult him often.

10. Don't overdo things.

❦ FINANCIER JOHN D. ROCKEFELLER'S
RULES OF LIVING FORMULATED AT AGE
SIXTY—WHICH HE FOLLOWED UNTIL HIS
DEATH MORE THAN THIRTY YEARS LATER

He who knows
others is learned;
he who knows
himself is wise.

☙ PHILOSOPHER LAO-TZU

Eighty years old!
No eyes left, no ears,
no teeth, no legs,
no wind! And when
all is said and done,
how astonishingly well
one does without them!

❦ POET PAUL CLAUDEL

N<small>O</small>, I haven't found any pattern at all to life itself, but then there probably is none other than birth and growth, decay and death, something we all know from the start.

❦ WRITER GORE VIDAL,
WRITTEN ON HIS SIXTY-NINTH BIRTHDAY

I'll never make the
mistake of being
seventy again.

❦ BASEBALL MANAGER CASEY STENGEL

I look at my shadow over
  and over in the lake;
I see no white face,
  only the white hair,
I have lost my youth, and
  shall never find it again.
Useless to stir the lake-water!

❧ POET PO CHÜ-I

My yesterdays walk with me. They keep step, they are faces that peer over my shoulder.

❧ WRITER WILLIAM GOLDING

Nothing, of course, begins at the time you think it did.

❦ WRITER LILLIAN HELLMAN

I have a simple
philosophy:
Fill what's empty.
Empty what's full.
And scratch where
it itches.

❦ SOCIALITE ALICE ROOSEVELT
LONGWORTH

Only of one thing
I am sure: When I
dream, I am always
ageless.

❦ POET ELIZABETH COATSWORTH

Nothing depresses me anymore. For a while in your life you worry about the passage of time and getting old and . . . after a while you just say, "My God, does it matter? Get on with it."

❦ MUSICIAN BOBBY SHORT

Literally thousands of wonderful friends have accompanied me in life, and many now await me in the secret eternity to come. I have enjoyed the long voyage.

❧ PHOTOGRAPHER ANSEL ADAMS

Lots of old people don't get wise, but you don't get wise unless you age.

❦ SCHOLAR JOAN ERIKSON

What have I done
to achieve longevity?
Woken up each morning
and tried to remember
not to wear my hearing
aid in the bath.

❦ WRITER/ACTOR ROBERT MORLEY

We ourselves feel that what we are doing is just a drop in the ocean. But if that drop was not in the ocean, I think the ocean would be less because of that missing drop.

❦ HUMANITARIAN MOTHER TERESA

I really thought I could do something to change the world. I soon found out you can't change the world. The best you can do is learn to live with it.

❦ WRITER HENRY MILLER

Pray for the dead
and fight like hell
for the living.

❦ LABOR ACTIVIST MOTHER JONES

I don't like people who have never fallen or stumbled. Their virtue is lifeless and isn't of much value. Life hasn't revealed its beauty to them.

❧ WRITER BORIS PASTERNAK

The trick is growing up without growing old.

❦ BASEBALL MANAGER CASEY STENGEL

Life has taught me that it knows better plans than we can imagine, so that I try to submerge my own desires, apt to be too insistent, into a calm willingness to accept what comes, and to make the most of it, then wait again. I have discovered that there is a Pattern, larger and more beautiful than our short vision can weave. . . .

❦ WRITER JULIA SETON

ZEN STUDENT: "What happens after death?"

ZEN MASTER: "I do not know."

ZEN STUDENT: "How can that be? You are a Zen Master!"

ZEN MASTER: "But I am not a dead Zen Master."

❦ QUOTED BY RAM DASS

I don't look to jump
over seven-foot bars.
I look around for
one-foot bars that
I can step over.

❦ FINANCIER **WARREN BUFFETT**

A sign of growing old is when interviewers start asking you, "What would you do differently if you had your life to live over again?" I give some sort of answer because I don't wish to be rude, but I don't tell them the image that comes into my mind because they would think it vain and frivolous, and no one wants to be a subject for ridicule.

I see myself as a tall, skinny Fellini, vigorously lifting weights. That's what I would do differently. I would lift weights.

❧ DIRECTOR FEDERICO FELLINI

W hen you're through with sex, with ambition, what can an old man create? Art, of course, a piece of art that will go beyond him into the lives of young people, the people who haven't had time to create. The old man meets the young people and lives on.

❦ POET WILLIAM CARLOS WILLIAMS

While people keep waiting and waiting for something big to happen in life, the "now" is passing them by. Do you know how fast a "now" passes? At the rate of 186,000 miles per second, the speed of light. So no matter how much you love and enjoy a particular "now," that's how fast it becomes a "was." . . . That's why I never use the word "if" anymore. An "if" is a "never was."

❦ COMEDIAN SID CAESAR

When Goya was eighty
he drew an ancient man
propped on two sticks,
with a great mass of white
hair and beard all over his
face, and the inscription
"I am still learning."

❦ WRITER SIMONE DE BEAUVOIR

There are two things to aim at in life: first, to get what you want and, after that, to enjoy it. Only the wisest of mankind achieve the second.

❦ WRITER LOGAN PEARSALL SMITH

Life is a tragedy when seen in close-up, but a comedy in long shot.

❦ DIRECTOR/ACTOR CHARLIE CHAPLIN

Never contradict. Never explain. Never apologize. (Those are the secrets of a happy life.)

❧ NAVAL COMMANDER
JOHN ARBUTHNOT FISHER (BARON FISHER)

The man who works and is never bored is never old. Work and interest in worthwhile things are the best remedy for age. Each day I am reborn. Each day I must begin again.

❦ MUSICIAN PABLO CASALS

It's worth asking:
What do you want?
It gets harder to
answer as you get
older. The answer gets
subtler and subtler.

❦ WRITER JOHN JEROME

Human life—indeed all life—
is poetry. It's *we* who live it,
unconsciously, day by day, like
scenes in a play, yet in its inviolable
wholeness it lives *us,* it composes
us. This is something far different
from the old cliché "Turn your life
into a work of art"; we are works
of art—but we are not the artist.

❧ WRITER/PSYCHOANALYST
LOU ANDREAS-SALOMÉ

Dying is a very dull, dreary, affair. And my advice to you is to have nothing whatever to do with it.

❦ WRITER W. SOMERSET MAUGHAM, TO HIS NEPHEW ROBIN

A stockbroker urged me to buy a stock that would triple its value every year. I told him, "At my age, I don't even buy green bananas."

🍃 POLITICIAN CLAUDE PEPPER

If *A* is a success in life, then *A* equals *x* plus *y* plus *z*. Work is *x*; *y* is play; and *z* is keeping your mouth shut.

❧ PHYSICIST ALBERT EINSTEIN

Life is constantly providing
us with new funds, new
resources, even when we
are reduced to immobility.
In life's ledger there is no
such thing as frozen assets.

❦ WRITER HENRY MILLER

The older I get,
the greater power
I seem to have to
help the world; I am
like a snowball—the
further I am rolled,
the more I gain.

❦ FEMINIST SUSAN B. ANTHONY

ROY ACUFF *(1903–92)* U.S. country-and-western musician; called the "King of Country Music"

ANSEL ADAMS *(1902–84)* U.S. conservationist and photographer, known for expansive landscapes of the American West

MARIAN ANDERSON *(1902–93)* First African American to perform at New York's Metropolitan Opera; United Nations delegate; winner of Presidential Medal of Freedom

LOU ANDREAS-SALOMÉ *(1861–1937)* Russian writer and psychoanalyst with practice in Vienna; friend and colleague of the Freuds; companion to philosopher Friedrich Wilhelm Nietzsche and poet Rainer Maria Rilke

SUSAN B. ANTHONY *(1820–1906)* U.S. suffragist and social reformer; leader of the American women's suffrage movement; also involved in temperance and abolitionist movements

EVE ARDEN *(1909–90)* U.S. actress; starred in TV sitcom *Our Miss Brooks;* Academy Award nominee for supporting role in film classic *Mildred Pierce*

RICHARD ARMOUR *(1906–89)* U.S. writer and poet, best known for light verses on modern life and syndicated column "Armour's Armory"

LOUIS ARMSTRONG *(1900–71)* U.S. jazz trumpeter, singer, and innovator; appeared in more than fifty films; first major jazz virtuoso; called "Satchmo"

MARY KAY ASH *(c. 1920s–)* U.S. business executive; founded Mary Kay Cosmetics (world's largest direct-sales cosmetics company) with five thousand dollars

FRED ASTAIRE *(1899–1987)* U.S. dancer, actor, and singer; noted for debonair charm and grace; best known for his '30s films with Ginger Rogers, such as *Top Hat* and *The Gay Divorcee*

LADY NANCY ASTOR *(1879–1964)* American-born British politician; succeeded her husband as MP (member of Parliament); first woman to hold seat in British House of Commons; active in women's rights and temperance

DANIEL-FRANÇOIS-ESPRIT AUBER *(1782–1871)* French composer of operas *Masaniello* (or *La Muette de Portici*) and *Fra Diavolo*

LUCILLE BALL *(1911–89)* U.S. actress and comedian; most famous for her role in television's *I Love Lucy*, one of the most successful shows in history and which she produced with her husband, Desi Arnaz

TALLULAH BANKHEAD *(1903–68)* U.S. actress famous for husky voice, outrageous declamations, and unabashed lifestyle; plays: *The Little Foxes* and *The Skin of Our Teeth;* films: Hitchcock's *Lifeboat*

ETHEL BARRYMORE *(1879–1959)* Member of famed Barrymore acting clan; "First Lady of American Theater"; plays include *The Second Mrs. Tanqueray* and *The Corn is Green*

BERNARD BARUCH *(1870–1965)* U.S. financier, statesman, and presidential economic adviser; rose from office boy to successful banker through speculation

SAMUEL BECKETT *(1906–89)* Irish playwright and author; dealt with communication issues and life's futility *(Waiting for Godot);* 1969 Nobel Prize for literature

HARRY BELAFONTE *(1927–)* U.S. actor and singer; three Grammy Awards; first African American to win an Emmy; civil rights and political activist

SAUL BELLOW *(1915–)* Canadian-born U.S. writer
and professor (University of Chicago); novels: *Henderson
the Rain King, Herzog, Humboldt's Gift;* 1976 Nobel Prize
for literature

BERNARD BERENSON *(1865–1959)* U.S. art critic and
writer; a foremost authority on Italian Renaissance art

INGRID BERGMAN *(1915–82)* Swedish actress; star
of classics such as *Casablanca, Spellbound,* and *Notorious;*
seven-time Oscar nominee, three-time winner

EUBIE BLAKE *(1883–1983)* U.S. jazz, ragtime, and
boogie-woogie composer and pianist

JORGE LUIS BORGES *(1899–1986)* Argentine
writer whose use of fantasy *(Labyrinths)* had enormous
influence on world literature; went blind and became
director of the National Library

HAROLD BRODKEY *(1930–96)* U.S. writer;
completed 835-page novel *The Runaway Soul* twenty-
seven years after starting; later writings explored his
imminent death due to AIDS

MEL BROOKS *(1926–)* U.S. comedic movie director,
writer, and actor *(The Producers, Blazing Saddles,* and
Young Frankenstein); cowrote book and wrote music for
Tony Award–winning stage version of *The Producers*

JOHN BUCHAN, FIRST BARON TWEEDSMUIR
(1875–1940) Scottish statesman and writer of more
than fifty books; adventure novels and thrillers include
Prester John and *The Thirty-nine Steps*

PEARL S. BUCK *(1892–1973)* U.S. writer raised in
China who returned there as adult missionary; 1938
Nobel Prize for *The Good Earth*

BUDDHA *(c. 563–483 B.C.E.)* Founder of Buddhism;
son of a prince who forsook court for ascetic life;

received enlightenment, according to tradition, under a bodhi tree; spent the next forty years teaching; the name Buddha means "enlightened one"

WARREN BUFFETT *(1930–)* U.S. financier and billionaire; chairman and CEO of conglomerate Berkshire Hathaway, Inc.; known for focus on value investing and self-deprecating comments on his stock picks

LUIS BUÑUEL *(1900–83)* Spanish film director; work characterized by black humor and intense imagery *(That Obscure Object of Desire* and *The Discreet Charm of the Bourgeoisie)*

BILLIE BURKE *(1884–1970)* U.S. actress; Broadway musical-comedy star in 1900s; went on to films. Best known as Glinda the Good Witch in *The Wizard of Oz*

SID CAESAR *(1922–2001)* U.S. comedian; one of the groundbreaking writers and cast of TV sketch show *Your Show of Shows,* with Imogene Coca, Carl Reiner, and Mel Brooks

JOSEPH CAMPBELL *(1904–87)* U.S. writer on mythology and comparative religion *(The Hero with a Thousand Faces);* popularized by television appearances on PBS

FRANK CAPRA *(1897–1991)* Italian-born U.S. film director; delighted in the dignity and strength of common man (Oscar-winning *It Happened One Night, Mr. Deeds Goes to Town, You Can't Take It With You);* best known for Christmas classic *It's a Wonderful Life*

ANDREW CARNEGIE *(1835–1918)* Scottish-born American industrialist; went from factory hand to founder of the largest iron-and-steel works in the United States; as philanthropist, endowed numerous public institutions

EMILY CARR *(1871–1945)* One of Canada's
preeminent painters; began writing at age seventy

JIMMY CARTER *(1924–)* Thirty-ninth U.S. president,
remembered for Camp David peace agreements; headed
family's peanut business, then entered politics; governor
of Georgia. Active in world politics as negotiator;
humanitarian

LILLIAN CARTER *(1898–1983)* "Miss Lillian," mother
of U.S. president Jimmy Carter; joined Peace Corps
at age sixty-eight and worked as nurse in India

PABLO CASALS *(1876–1973)* Spanish cellist,
composer, conductor, and pianist; founded Barcelona
Orchestra; left Spain at outset of Spanish Civil War;
settled in France; performed until age ninety

SÉBASTIEN ROCH NICOLAS CHAMFORT
(1740–94) French playwright and conversationalist
whose witty maxims became popular during the
French Revolution

RAYMOND CHANDLER *(1888–1959)* U.S. writer;
preeminent detective novelist *(The Big Sleep; Farewell,
My Lovely; The Long Goodbye);* created private eye
Philip Marlowe

WILLIAM ELLERY CHANNING *(1780–1841)* U.S.
clergyman, famous for sermons at Congregational
Federal Street Church in Boston; eventually became
Unitarian leader

CHARLIE CHAPLIN *(1889–1977)* English actor and
director; king of silent comedy; left the United States in
'50s because of left-wing politics; settled in Switzerland;
knighted in 1975

SIR FRANCIS CHICHESTER *(1901–72)* English
adventurer badly hurt in a plane crash; took up

yachting. Successfully sailed solo around the world in 1966–67; knighted upon return to England

JULIA CHILD *(1912–)* U.S. chef, food writer, and television host; popularized French cooking on hit TV show and in numerous cookbooks

AGATHA CHRISTIE *(1891–1976)* English mystery writer, considered by many to be queen of the mystery novel. Wrote more than seventy novels, many short stories, and plays; created Hercule Poirot and Miss Jane Marple

CHUANG-TZU (CHUANG CHOU), *(c. 369–c. 286 B.C.E.)* Chinese Taoist philosopher and hermit; offered a prime ministership, reportedly turned it down, saying, "I prefer the enjoyment of my own free will."

SIR WINSTON CHURCHILL *(1874–1965)* English statesman; won election to Parliament in 1900 but regarded as has-been by the 1930s. In 1940 formed coalition government that led the British to victory against initially terrible odds over Axis powers. Celebrated as the last of the classic orators

CICERO (MARCUS TULLIUS CICERO), *(106–43 B.C.E.)* Roman orator and statesman; foiled plot by Catiline to seize Roman Republic; wrote rhetorical and philosophical works; killed by henchmen of his enemy Marc Antony

PAUL CLAUDEL *(1868–1955)* French poet *(Cinq Grandes Odes)*, essayist, playwright *(Partage de Midi)*, and opera librettist *(Jeanne d'Arc au bûcher)*; leading voice of French Catholic literature

GEORGES CLEMENCEAU *(1841–1929)* French statesman and journalist; dubbed "the Tiger" for his toughmindedness; presided at 1919 Peace Conference

ELIZABETH COATSWORTH *(1893–1986)* U.S. poet, children's author; won Newbery Award for *The Cat Who Went to Heaven*

COLETTE *(1873–1954)* French novelist (the *Claudine* series, *Chéri*, and *Gigi*), memoirist; famous for her bohemianism; worked in acting troupes, as mime and dancer

CONFUCIUS (K'UNG-FU-TZU), *(c. 551–479 B.C.E.)* Chinese philosopher; civil servant who became wandering sage and teacher; ideas collected in the *Analects;* basic tenets include promotion of moral values, emphasis on social control

SEAN CONNERY *(1930–)* Scottish actor, considered by many to be definitive James Bond; other movies: *The Man Who Would Be King, The Molly Maguires, The Untouchables*

CAMILLE COROT *(1796–1875)* French landscape painter

MALCOLM COWLEY *(1898–1989)* U.S. editor, critic, and writer; as literary editor of *The New Republic*, discovered John Cheever and resurrected William Faulkner's career

JOAN CRAWFORD (BORN LUCILLE LE SUEUR), *(1904–77)* U.S. film actress: *The Women, Mildred Pierce* (for which she won an Oscar), and *Whatever Happened to Baby Jane?*

QUENTIN CRISP *(1908–99)* English writer, known for acerbic bon mots and unabashed homosexuality. Became camp icon, particularly for his memoir, *The Naked Civil Servant*

HUME CRONYN *(1911–)* Versatile Canadian stage actor most adept at portrayals of "ordinary" people, later carried this success to numerous screen roles. Husband of the late actress Jessica Tandy

CROWFOOT (ISAPO-MUXIKA), *(c. 1826–90)* Chief of the Blackfoot (Native American) confederacy; noted peacemaker in tribal disputes

MARIE CURIE *(1867–1934)* Polish-born French scientist; isolated radium and polonium; joint winner of Nobel Prize for physics in 1903; winner Nobel Prize for chemistry in 1911

RODNEY DANGERFIELD *(1921–)* U.S. stand-up and film comedian known for tag line "I get no respect"; began his career at age fifteen, but didn't become a success until age forty

CLARENCE DARROW *(1857–1938)* U.S. attorney; gained prominence for defense work on high-profile Scopes trial (should evolution be taught?) and Leopold and Loeb murder trial

CHARLES DARWIN *(1809–82)* English naturalist; outlined theory of evolution by natural selection in *Origin of Species,* after voyage on HMS *Beagle* as ship's naturalist

RAM DASS (BORN RICHARD ALPERT), *(1933–)* U.S. writer, teacher, and humanitarian; researched LSD at Harvard; studied yoga in India; created spiritual support foundation and cofounded international aid group

BETTE DAVIS *(1908–89)* U.S. film actress, known for feisty personality as well as for dramatic ability. Nominated ten times for Academy Award, won twice—for *Dangerous* and *Jezebel*

SIMONE DE BEAUVOIR *(1908–86)* French novelist, essayist, existentialist, and feminist *(The Second Sex)*

RUBY DEE *(1924–)* U.S. stage *(Raisin in the Sun),* film *(The Jackie Robinson Story, Do the Right Thing)* and television actress; published novelist, poet, and columnist;

civil rights activist; winner of Frederick Douglass Award
from New York's Urban League with husband, actor
Ossie Davis

KIRK DOUGLAS *(1916–)* U.S. actor *(Spartacus)*,
director, writer (novels and two autobiographies);
as a civic activist, awarded the Legion of Honor and
the Presidential Medal of Freedom

W. E. B. DUBOIS *(1868–1963)* U.S. writer
(The Souls of Black Folk) and educator; cofounded
the National Association for the Advancement of
Colored People (NAACP)

WILL DURANT *(1885–1981)* U.S. historian and essayist;
eleven-volume work *The Story of Civilization* covers
civilization from prehistory to the nineteenth century

LEO DUROCHER *(1905–91)* U.S. baseball player
(shortstop, seventeen years); then twenty-four seasons
as major league manager. Elected to National Baseball
Hall of Fame in 1994

GERALD DURRELL *(1925–95)* English writer and
naturalist; on the Island of Jersey founded his own zoo
dedicated to breeding endangered species; wrote on
animal conservation and collecting

CLINT EASTWOOD *(1930–)* U.S. actor (major box-
office draw as a "tough guy"); director (Oscar-winner
Unforgiven) and producer

MARIE EBNER-ESCHENBACH *(1830–1916)*
Austrian writer; achieved fame and distinction
with novels of "poetic realism," most notably
The Two Countesses

ALBERT EINSTEIN *(1879–1955)* German-Swiss-
American physicist; formulated theories of relativity;
urged international control for nuclear weapons

GEORGE ELIOT (MARY ANN EVANS), *(1819–80)* English novelist *(Middlemarch, Daniel Deronda);* works captured England's rural and lower middle class, particularly of the Midlands

JOAN ERIKSON *(1902–97)* Canadian-born U.S. authority on human development; with husband, Erik, coformulated Eriksonian life-cycle theory on progression of personal identity

WILLIAM FAULKNER *(1897–1962)* U.S. writer; immortalized home state of Mississippi in lyrical novels set in imaginary Yoknapatawpha County. Won Nobel Prize for literature in 1949

FEDERICO FELLINI *(1920–93)* Italian film director *(I Vitelloni* and *La Strada);* four Oscars

MILLICENT FENWICK *(1910–92)* Outspoken U.S. politician; served as member of U.S. House of Representatives (R, NJ) from 1975 through 1982

RICHARD P. FEYNMAN *(1918–88)* U.S. physicist; worked on first atomic bomb; advanced quantum electrodynamics; won Nobel Prize in 1965; popularized science in humorous lectures and books

DIETRICH FISCHER-DIESKAU *(1925–)* German operatic baritone; one of the best-known interpreters of German lieder, including song cycles of Schubert

JOHN ARBUTHNOT FISHER (BARON FISHER), *(1841–1920)* British naval commander; born in Ceylon, became First Sea Lord; introduced dreadnought battleships; revolutionized British naval training

ELLA FITZGERALD *(1918–96)* U.S. jazz singer; raised in orphanage; at 16, entered talent contest where she caught bandleader Chick Webb's eye; helped develop scat-singing

BERNARD LE BOVIER DE FONTENELLE
(1657–1757) French writer and centenarian; famed
for trying his hand at a wide range of literature—
including satires, essays, tragedies, dialogues, idylls,
and histories

ANATOLE FRANCE (JACQUES-ANATOLE
FRANÇOIS THIBAULT), *(1844–1924)* French
writer (*Thaïs,* a novel of post-classical Alexandria,
and modern fable *Penguin Island*); Nobel Prize for
literature in 1921

VICTOR FRANKL *(1905–97)* Austrian psychiatrist;
survivor of Nazi death camp; developed theory
of logotherapy—human motivation comes from a
"will to meaning"; professor; author of thirty-two
books; avid mountain climber and pilot

BENJAMIN FRANKLIN *(1706–90)* U.S. statesman,
scientist; made fortune as printer in Philadelphia, then
devoted himself to science and U.S. independence;
Revolutionary representative in Paris; president of the
state of Pennsylvania; delegate during framing of U.S.
Constitution

ROBERT FROST *(1874–1963)* U.S. poet, known
as "the voice of New England"; taught at Amherst
College and Harvard; won three Pulitzer Prizes
(1924, 1931, and 1937)

J. PAUL GETTY *(1892–1976)* U.S. oil magnate,
who inherited $15 million and, by shrewd acquisitions,
transformed himself into a billionaire; also famed for
his art collection

SIR JOHN GIELGUD *(1904–2000)* British actor;
leading Shakespearean; won Academy Award for
portrayal of dying butler in *Arthur*

DIZZY GILLESPIE (JOHN BIRKS), *(1917–93)*
U.S. jazz trumpeter, composer, and bandleader; leading developer and artist of bebop

HERMIONE GINGOLD *(1897–1987)* British actress famous for tart comedic portrayals on stage and screen, notably in film *Gigi*

JOHANN WOLFGANG VON GOETHE *(1749–1832)* German writer, scientist, court official; initially a Romantic poet; in later years completed his masterpiece *Faust* about a man who makes a pact with the devil

WILLIAM GOLDING *(1911–93)* British novelist *(Lord of the Flies);* Nobel Prize for literature in 1983

RUTH GORDON *(1896–1985)* Actress, playwright, screenwriter (often wrote with husband Garson Kanin); won Academy Award for portrayal of a Manhattan witch in *Rosemary's Baby*

MAURICE GOUDEKET *(1889–1977)* French writer; perhaps best known as the third (and most-loved) husband of writer Colette; examined aging in his book *The Delights of Growing Old*

MARTHA GRAHAM *(1893–1991)* U.S. modern dancer, innovator, and choreographer; founder of Martha Graham Dance Company; received Presidential Medal of Freedom in 1976

WALTER GROPIUS *(1883–1969)* German-born U.S. architect; formed functional modernist "Bauhaus School," which celebrated simple lines, utilizing glass and metal

DASHIELL HAMMETT *(1894–1961)* Former Pinkerton detective and U.S. writer who defined the hard-boiled detective novel *(The Maltese Falcon)*

HELEN HAYES *(1900–93)* U.S. stage and screen actress; won Academy Award for first screen role in

The Sin of Madelon Claudet in 1931; won second
Academy Award in 1970 *(Airport)*

JOSEPH HELLER *(1923–99)* U.S. writer best
known for antiwar novel *Catch-22* and other works
characterized by a sense of the absurd

LILLIAN HELLMAN *(1906–84)* U.S. playwright
(The Children's Hour) and memoirist *(Pentimento* and
Scoundrel Time)

KATHARINE HEPBURN *(1907–)* U.S. actress; star of
numerous Hollywood hits *(Bringing Up Baby, The African
Queen* and *On Golden Pond);* four Academy Awards

EDWARD HOAGLAND *(1932–)* U.S. novelist, essayist,
naturalist, and travel writer; passionate environmentalist

ERIC HOFFER *(1902–83)* U.S. writer, philosopher,
longshoreman; known for powerful writings on social
order; awarded Presidential Medal of Freedom in 1983

OLIVER WENDELL HOLMES JR. *(1841–1935)*
U.S. judge and legal theorist; wrote definitive text on
common law; chief justice of the Massachusetts Supreme
Court; associate justice of the U.S. Supreme Court

OLIVER WENDELL HOLMES SR. *(1809–1894)*
U.S. physician and writer; first dean of Harvard Medical
School

VICTORIA HOLT *(1906–93)* British romance writer
dubbed the "Queen of Romantic Suspense"; first best-
seller was *Mistress of Mellyn* in 1960; continued writing
until her death

BOB HOPE *(1903–)* English-born U.S. actor and
comedian famous for rapid-fire wisecracks and quips;
active in humanitarian causes, particularly USO

GRACE MURRAY HOPPER *(1906–92)*
Mathematician and U.S. Navy Rear Admiral; early

computer programmer and software developer; won first
Computer Science Man-of-the-Year Award in 1969;
served as senior consultant to Digital Equipment Corp.
in her eighties

LENA HORNE *(1917–)* U.S. singer of blues and
ballads; began in chorus of Harlem's Cotton Club;
first African American to sign long-term Hollywood
contract

WILLIAM DEAN HOWELLS *(1837–1920)* U.S.
novelist and critic; as editor of *Atlantic Monthly* and
Harper's Magazine, influenced authors such as Mark Twain

VICTOR HUGO *(1802–85)* French poet and writer;
leader of French Romantic movement; best known for
panoramic social novel *Les Misérables;* also was active in
French politics

JOHN HUSTON *(1906–87)* U.S. actor, screenwriter, and
director (*The Maltese Falcon, The Treasure of Sierra Madre,*
and many other acclaimed films); characteristically a
hard-liver, he died on location at age eighty-one

WILLIAM RALPH INGE *(1860–1954)* English
theologian and prelate; professor of divinity at
Cambridge, later dean of St. Paul's; pessimistic sermons
earned him the nickname "The Gloomy Dean"

WASHINGTON IRVING *(1783–1859)* U.S. writer,
lawyer, and diplomat; famed for his *Sketch Book of
Geoffrey Crayon, Gent.,* which included "The Legend
of Sleepy Hollow" and other lighthearted looks at old
Dutch New York

CHRISTOPHER ISHERWOOD *(1904–86)* British-
born U.S. novelist; best-known works (*Berlin Stories,*
part of which inspired *Cabaret*) based on experiences
in decadent pre-Hitler Berlin

JOHN JEROME *(1935–)* U.S. magazine and book writer *(On Turning Sixty-five: Notes from the Field)*

ST. JEROME (SOPHRONIUS EUSEBIUS HIERONYMUS), *(c. 342–420)* Roman Catholic Church Father; in 386 settled in Bethlehem, where he wrote influential biblical commentaries and Vulgate version of Bible

MOTHER JONES (MARY HARRIS JONES), *(c. 1837–1930)* Irish-born U.S. labor activist; following death of husband and four children, became organizer for United Mine Workers of America; publicized evils of child labor

JUVENAL (DECIMUS JUNIUS JUVENALIS), *(c. 55–c. 140)* Roman satirist and lawyer celebrated for witty verse on Roman mores and vices; much translated

ELIA KAZAN *(1909–)* Turkish-born U.S. stage and film director; cofounded Actor's Studio (propounding "method acting"); directed film classics such as *On the Waterfront* and *A Streetcar Named Desire*

HELEN KELLER *(1880–1968)* U.S writer *(The Story of My Life)* and lecturer; blind and deaf at nineteen months; Presidential Medal of Freedom, 1967

DOROTHEA KENT *(1916–90)* U.S. actress, primarily in silents, film comedy shorts, and early talkies

OMAR KHAYYÁM (OR UMAR KHAYYÁM), *(c. 1048–1122)* Persian poet, mathematician, and astronomer; known primarily in the East for scientific accomplishments, in the West, for his *Rubáiyát,* translated by Edward FitzGerald

KIM CHONG-GU *(c. fifteenth to sixteenth century)* Korean poet, widely read during the reign of the tyrant Yonsangun

B.B. KING (RILEY B.), *(1928–)* U.S. blues singer and guitarist with powerful influence on rock; born to sharecropper parents; rhythm-and-blues hits include *Live at the Regal*

JUDITH KRANTZ *(1928–)* U.S. novelist; best-selling contemporary romances include *Scruples*

RAY KROC *(1902–84)* U.S. business executive; initially a milk-shake salesman, bought the name McDonald's from brothers who owned a drive-in restaurant; with name, created worldwide chain and became father of fast food

DR. ELISABETH KÜBLER-ROSS *(1926–)* U.S./Swiss psychiatrist, specializing in care of the terminally ill; achieved worldwide acclaim with first book, *On Death and Dying*

MAGGIE KUHN *(1905–95)* U.S. activist; at age sixty-five, founded the Gray Panthers to address the problems of ageism

STANLEY KUNITZ *(1905–89)* Poet Laureate of the United States; taught at New School for Social Research and Columbia University

KARL LAGERFELD *(1939–)* Influential German-born French fashion designer; designed for Chloe and Chanel, as well as his eponymous line

ANN LANDERS (ESTHER PAULINE "EPPIE" FRIEDMAN), *(1918–)* U.S. syndicated advice columnist; twin of fellow sob sister Abigail Van Buren ("Dear Abby")

LAO-TZU *(c. 604–531 B.C.E.)* Chinese philosopher (name means "old master"); his *Tao-te-ching,* compiled three hundred years after his death, teaches simplicity, detachment, going with the flow of nature

GYPSY ROSE LEE (ROSE LOUISE HOVICK), *(1914–70)* U.S. stripper; became a queen of burlesque with her teasing act

MADELEINE L'ENGLE *(1918–)* U.S. novelist and children's book writer; won Newbery Award for *A Wrinkle in Time*

MAX LERNER *(1902–92)* U.S. journalist and political theorist; initially a leftist and spokesman for Popular Front; became a critic of New Left in later years

DORIS LESSING *(1919–)* Rhodesian-born writer *(The Grass Is Singing* and *The Golden Notebook)*

ANNE MORROW LINDBERGH *(1906–2001)* U.S. poet, memoirist, aviator; assisted husband, Charles Lindbergh, in charting international air routes; books include *Gift from the Sea; Hour of Gold, Hour of Lead*

HENRY WADSWORTH LONGFELLOW *(1807–82)* U.S. poet and professor of modern languages and literature at Harvard; gained contemporary fame with romantic stories in verse, most notably *Hiawatha*

ALICE ROOSEVELT LONGWORTH *(1884–1981)* U.S. socialite and darling of D.C. society; daughter of President Theodore Roosevelt; called "Princess Alice"; known for acerbic wit, independence, and vivacity

CLARE BOOTHE LUCE *(1903–87)* U.S. diplomat and politician; member of U.S. House of Representatives, then U.S. ambassador to Italy; received Presidential Medal of Freedom

HORATIO LURO *(1926–)* Argentine-born horse trainer; known as "El Gran Señor"; inducted into the National Museum of Racing Hall of Fame

MAURICE MAETERLINCK *(1862–1949)* Belgian writer of symbolist poetry, plays, and popular expositions on scientific subjects; awarded Nobel Prize for literature in 1911

THOMAS MANN *(1875–1955)* German novelist born into a patrician family; first celebrated novel *Buddenbrooks* traces the decline of similar family; early opponent of Nazism, settled in the United States; won Nobel Prize for literature in 1929

GROUCHO (JULIUS HENRY) MARX *(1890–1977)* Wisecracking, cigar-wielding, cowriting member of the Marx Brothers; host of TV's *You Bet Your Life*

HARPO (ARTHUR) MARX *(1888–1964)* Silent, curly-haired master of mimicry in Marx Brothers comedy team; master harpist; finally "talked" in autobiography *Harpo Speaks*

W. (WILLIAM) SOMERSET MAUGHAM *(1874–1965)* British writer best known for short stories and partly autobiographical novel, *Of Human Bondage*. Led an adventurous life; served as a British secret agent in both world wars

BARBARA MCCLINTOCK *(1902–92)* U.S. geneticist and botanist, known for groundbreaking work in cytogenetics. Awarded Nobel Prize in physiology or medicine in 1983—first woman to win unshared Nobel Prize

MARGARET MEAD *(1901–78)* U.S. anthropologist and American Museum of Natural History curator; known for influential study *Coming of Age in Samoa*

GOLDA MEIR *(1898–1978)* Israeli minister of labor, minister of foreign affairs, then first female prime minister. Emigrated to Palestine from Milwaukee, Wisconsin; active in fight for Israeli independence

MENCIUS (MENG-TZU), *(372–289 B.C.E.)* Chinese philosopher and cofounder of Confucianism; advocated social and political reform, humanitarianism. After death, teachings collected into *The Book of Meng-tzu*

GIAN-CARLO MENOTTI *(1911–)* Italian-born U.S. composer, best known for series of operas beginning with *Amelia Goes to the Ball;* founded Festival of Two Worlds in Spoleto, Italy, in 1958

YEHUDI MENUHIN *(1916–1999)* U.S.–born British violin virtuoso; appeared at age seven with San Francisco Symphony; founded school for musically gifted children in Surrey, England

HENRY MILLER *(1891–1980)* U.S. writer famous for bohemian semiautobiographical novels (*Tropic of Cancer, Sexus,* etc.)

JOAQUIN MILLER (PEN NAME OF CINCINNATUS HEINE MILLER), *(1837–1913)* American writer with "classic" frontier lifestyle: miner, soldier, farmer, judge

JESSICA MITFORD *(1917–96)* U.S. writer, born in England. Social critic, known for investigative studies *(The American Way of Death);* wrote celebrated autobiography *(Daughters and Rebels)* of unconventional Mitford way of life

FRANÇOIS MITTERRAND *(1916–96)* Leader of French socialists in 1970s; president of France in 1980s

PIERRE MONTEUX *(1875–1964)* French-American conductor; conducted Diaghilev's Ballet Russe; also Metropolitan Opera, and Boston, Amsterdam, San Francisco, and London Symphony Orchestras

ROBERT MORLEY *(1908–92)* British actor (Henry Higgins in *Pygmalion,* Sheridan Whiteside in *The Man Who Came to Dinner*); writer of plays and books; appeared in more than sixty films *(The African Queen, Around the World in 80 Days)*

JOHN MORTIMER *(1923–)* English barrister and
writer, best known for novels featuring Horace Rumpole,
a middle-aged defense barrister

GRANDMA MOSES (ANNA MARY ROBERTSON),
(1860–1961) U.S. self-taught "primitive" artist; began
painting simple, mostly rural scenes in her seventies;
achieved worldwide fame

MALCOLM MUGGERIDGE *(1903–90)* English
print and TV journalist who characterized his life as
a spiritual journey toward a greater understanding of
faith; became a Roman Catholic in 1982

HELEN NEARING *(1904–95)* U.S. writer; involved
with philosopher Krishnamurti. Married radical Scott
Nearing, settled on Vermont farm, and became advocate
of simple living

LOUISE NEVELSON *(1899–1988)* Russian-born
American sculptor and printmaker, famed for
"environmental" pieces using painted boxes and wood,
plexiglass and metal

SIR ISAAC NEWTON *(1642–1727)* English scientist
and mathematician; developed differential calculus;
formulated theory of gravitation; wrote on optics

JACK NICKLAUS *(1940–)* U.S. golfer known as the
"Golden Bear"; won first of four U.S. Opens in 1962;
also three British Opens, five PGA, and six U.S. Masters
championships; golf-course architect

SHERWIN B. NULAND *(1930–)* U.S. doctor,
surgeon, professor of surgery at Yale University. First
book, *How We Die,* won National Book Award

SEAN O'CASEY *(1884–1964)* Irish playwright;
born in a poor section of Dublin, worked as a laborer
before becoming a playwright; first plays dealt with

life of the poor; later plays more experimental and impressionistic

LAURENCE OLIVIER *(1907–89)* British actor and director; leading classical and Shakespearean actor of his time; romantic lead in Hollywood films such as *Wuthering Heights* and *Rebecca*. Knighted in 1947, made peer in 1971

ARISTOTLE ONASSIS *(1906–75)* Greek shipping tycoon, born in Smyrna, Turkey; pioneer in supertankers. Had long relationship with diva Maria Callas; married former first lady Jacqueline Kennedy

IRIS ORIGO *(1902–)* Irish-born historian, biographer, and writer; created hospital and school for disadvantaged children on Italian estate; 1972 National Book Award for *Images and Shadows*

SATCHEL PAIGE *(1906–82)* U.S. baseball star; Negro League pitcher; joined majors in 1948 as oldest rookie to play major league baseball. At age fifty-nine, the oldest man to pitch in a major league game; elected to National Baseball Hall of Fame in 1971

BORIS PASTERNAK *(1890–1960)* Russian writer; lyric poet; translator of Shakespeare into Russian; famous novel *Dr. Zhivago* criticized the impact of the Soviet revolution. Refused Nobel Prize in 1958

NORMAN VINCENT PEALE *(1898–1993)* U.S. Christian Reformed pastor, lecturer, writer *(The Power of Positive Thinking)*

CLAUDE PEPPER *(1900–89)* U.S. senator and congressman from Florida; defended Social Security; worked for elderly's rights

PABLO PICASSO *(1881–1973)* Spanish painter *(Guernica, Three Musicians)* sculptor, Cubism pioneer; famed for artistic innovation and versatility

T. BOONE PICKENS *(1928–)* U.S. businessman; founder and president of Mesa Petroleum Co.; leading stock-market expert; descendant of Daniel Boone

BELVA PLAIN *(1919–)* U.S. writer; first novel, *Evergreen,* stayed on the *New York Times* best-seller list forty-one weeks. Has written nineteen novels; more than 25 million copies in print

PLATO *(c. 428–c. 348 B.C.E.)* Athenian philosopher; pupil of Socrates and teacher of Aristotle

PO CHÜ-I *(772–846)* Chinese lyric poet who lived during era of Tang dynasty; born in Honan, later governor of the province; poetry so esteemed it was engraved on stone tablets by imperial order

SIDNEY POITIER *(1927–)* U.S. actor *(In the Heat of the Night; To Sir With Love)* and director; first African-American movie star (Oscar nominee, *The Defiant Ones);* won Oscar for *Lilies of the Field*

J. B. PRIESTLEY *(1894–1984)* English playwright *(An Inspector Calls),* novelist *(The Good Companions* and *Angel Pavement),* and essayist

SAM RAYBURN *(1882–1961)* U.S. Congressman from Texas, re-elected twenty-four consecutive times; Speaker of the House for seventeen years, served longer in that post than any other politician

DELLA REESE *(1931–)* U.S. actress and singer; began singing gospel with Mahalia Jackson at age thirteen; first African-American woman to host national talk show; now best known for her role on TV's *Touched by an Angel*

JOHN CHARLES WALSHAM REITH (LORD REITH OR FIRST BARON REITH OF STONEHAVEN), *(1889–1971)* British engineer, broadcaster, and politician; headed BBC; member of Parliament, and Minister of Works

AGNES REPPLIER *(1855–1950)* U.S. essayist and biographer of major Catholic figures including Mère Marie of the Ursulines and Père Marquette; wrote for more than sixty-five years

DEBBIE REYNOLDS *(1932–)* U.S. actress known for "girl next door" roles in musicals and light comedy such as *Singin' in the Rain*

JEAN RHYS (PSEUDONYM OF GWEN WILLIAMS), *(1894–1979)* Caribbean-born British writer, celebrated for novels *(Wide Sargasso Sea)* about women trying to live without support

DON RICKLES *(1926–)* U.S. comedian, "king of the insult"; also dramatic and comedic film actor

EDWARD G. ROBINSON *(1893–1973)* Bucharest-born U.S. actor of stage and screen; hard-bitten portrayals of underworld characters *(Little Caesar)* won fame

JOHN D. ROCKEFELLER *(1839–1937)* U.S. oil magnate and philanthropist; founded Standard Oil Company and the Rockefeller Foundation "to promote the well-being of man-kind"

ANDY ROONEY *(1919–)* U.S. journalist; curmudgeonly commentator on life's foibles on television's *60 Minutes*

ELEANOR ROOSEVELT *(1884–1962)* American humanitarian, writer, first lady; served as delegate to the U.N. Assembly and chairperson of U.N. Human Rights Commission

JEAN ROSTAND *(1894–1977)* French biologist and essayist; known as the "venerable dean of biological generalists"

ARTUR RUBINSTEIN *(1887–1982)* Polish-born pianist; studied with Paderewski; toured Europe in the early 1900s; after World War II, lived in the United States

BERTRAND RUSSELL *(1872–1970)* British philosopher, famed for landmark logic and mathematics work *Principia Mathematica* and work in epistemology; political and social activist

JONAS SALK *(1914–95)* U.S. virologist; developed "Salk vaccine" to fight polio; was director of Salk Institute of San Diego

GEORGE SAND (PSEUDONYM OF AMANDINE LUCIE AURORE DUPIN, BARONNE DUDEVANT), *(1804–76)* French writer; scandalized society with unconventional manners and early erotic works; later works: studies of rustic life and autobiography

GEORGE SANTAYANA *(1863–1952)* Spanish philosopher; Harvard professor; spent last years in Roman convent, the guest of nuns. A naturalistic skeptical philosopher, nevertheless devoted to Catholic Church

MAY SARTON *(1912–95)* Highly prolific U.S. writer; fifty-three books include novels, nonfiction, and poetry; best known are her journals

ARTHUR SCHOPENHAUER *(1788–1860)* German philosopher, champion of the idea of the will. Lived for the most part in seclusion with his poodle; ideas finally caught on during last decade of his life

ALBERT SCHWEITZER *(1875–1965)* Alsatian missionary, theologian, musician, and philosopher who founded hospital in French equatorial Africa; won Nobel Peace Prize in 1952

FLORIDA SCOTT-MAXWELL *(1883–1979)* U.S. writer, Jungian psychologist. Books often focus on psychological issues, as in *Toward Relationships* and *The Measure of My Days*

SENECA (LUCIUS ANNAEUS SENECA) *(c. 4 B.C.E.–c. 65 C.E.)* Roman Stoic philosopher, tragedian; tutored Roman emperor Nero, who later condemned him; committed suicide in the calm Stoic manner

JULIA SETON *(1889–1975)* U.S. writer; most famous for work with husband, naturalist and Woodcraft League (precursor to Boy Scouts) founder Ernest Thompson Seton, and her biography of him, *By 1,000 Fires*

GEORGE BERNARD SHAW *(1856–1950)* Anglo-Irish playwright *(Man and Superman, Heartbreak House, Back to Methuselah),* critic, essayist, political activist; Nobel Prize for literature in 1925

BOBBY SHORT *(1926–)* U.S. pianist and singer with urbane, smooth style; "the Astaire of saloon singers"

JEAN SIBELIUS *(1865–1957)* Finnish composer, famed for symphonic poems based on the Finnish epic *Kalevala; Finlandia* is his most notable work

GEORGES SIMENON *(1903–89)* Belgian-French writer of detective novels; one of the most prolific and widely published writers of the twentieth century

ISAAC BASHEVIS SINGER *(1904–91)* Polish-born U.S. writer who won Nobel Prize in 1978 for poignant novels and short stories, all written in Yiddish, chronicling Jewish life in Poland and the United States

LOGAN PEARSALL SMITH *(1865–1946)* U.S.–born writer of short stories and essays who lived much of his life in England; produced books of criticism

SMOHALLA *(c. 1815–1907)* Wanapun (Native American) prophet; advocated a religion in which Native Americans would return to old way of life; followers were called "the Dreamers"

SOPHOCLES *(c. 496–405 B.C.E.)* Athenian playwright who wrote into his nineties; most famous for masterpiece *Oedipus Tyrannus;* besides tragedy, wrote satire, but only one of the latter remains

MURIEL SPARK *(1918–)* Scottish writer who has also lived in Rome and New York; wrote biographical studies, poetry, but best known for novels, namely *The Prime of Miss Jean Brodie*

FREYA STARK *(1893–1993)* British travel writer; called "the female Lawrence of Arabia," traveled extensively through the Middle East by herself

GLORIA STEINEM *(1934–)* U.S. journalist, writer, and women's rights activist; cofounder of *Ms.* magazine; helped organize National Women's Political Caucus

CASEY STENGEL *(1889–1975)* U.S. baseball player and manager; played for Brooklyn Dodgers; as manager, led New York Yankees to seven World Series victories; later managed the New York Mets. Famous for colorful way of speaking

JIMMY STEWART *(1908–97)* U.S. actor known for "everyman" roles; won Academy Award for role in *The Philadelphia Story;* served as bomber pilot during World War II; earned the Presidential Medal of Freedom

I. F. (ISIDOR FEINSTEIN) STONE *(1907–89)* U.S. journalist, publisher, social reformer; started his own political paper, *I. F. Stone's Weekly,* in 1953; attacked McCarthyism, racial discrimination, and the Vietnam War

AUGUST STRINDBERG *(1849–1912)* Swedish playwright and novelist, considered greatest modern Swedish writer; led tortured life, with three failed marriages, bouts of persecution mania, and, finally, a mystical conversion

HERBERT BAYARD SWOPE *(1892–1958)* U.S. journalist; executive editor of *New York World;* as reporter, won Pulitzer prize for articles from Germany in 1916; created the newspaper op-ed page

RABINDRANATH TAGORE *(1861–1941)* Indian poet, novelist, and philosopher; founded school blending Eastern and Western philosophies and educational systems; won Nobel Prize for literature in 1913

JESSICA TANDY *(1909–94)* London-born actress; won first Tony Award for her role as Blanche Dubois in *A Streetcar Named Desire;* Academy Award for *Driving Miss Daisy;* earned law degree in 1974

ELIZABETH TAYLOR *(1932–)* London-born American actress, winner of two Academy Awards *(Who's Afraid of Virginia Woolf* and *Butterfield 8);* outspoken AIDS activist

EDWARD TELLER *(1908–)* Hungarian-born American physicist, known as "the Father of the H-bomb" for work in nuclear physics; later active in social issues

MOTHER TERESA (AGNES GONXHA BOJAXHIU), *(1910–97)* Albanian Roman Catholic nun and humanitarian famed for her sisterhood dedicated to helping the poor, most notably in Calcutta, India; won Nobel Peace Prize in 1979

LEWIS THOMAS *(1913–93)* U.S pathologist; dean of Yale and New York University medical schools and president then chancellor of the Memorial Sloan-Kettering Cancer Center; wrote poetry, scientific papers, and essays, including those in National Book Award–winner *The Lives of a Cell*

LEO TOLSTOY *(1828–1910)* Russian writer and moralist; pioneer of "psychological novel" *(War and Peace,*

Anna Karenina). Stint in Crimean War inspired antiwar attitudes; later turned over his fortune to wife and lived as a peasant

HARRY S TRUMAN *(1884–1972)* Thirty-third president of the United States; haberdasher; entered politics in 1922; presidency marked by such important decisions as dropping the atom bomb, containing communism, the Berlin airlift, NATO, and the Marshall Plan

SOPHIE TUCKER *(1884–1966)* Russian-born U.S. singer and vaudeville entertainer; "the last of the red hot mamas." Never retired; on stage for sixty-two years; known for bawdy jokes, suggestive songs, and belting ability

MARK TWAIN (PSEUDONYM FOR SAMUEL LANGHORNE CLEMENS), *(1835–1910)* U.S. writer *(Tom Sawyer* and *Huckleberry Finn);* preeminent nineteenth-century American humorist and satirist

GORE VIDAL *(1925–)* U.S. novelist *(Julian, Burr,* and *Lincoln),* playwright, and acidic essayist on American life

FRANÇOIS MARIE AROUET DE VOLTAIRE *(1694–1778)* French philosopher, writer, and scathing satirist *(Candide);* principal champion of European Enlightenment

SAM WALTON *(1918–92)* U.S. businessman, founded Wal-Mart and built it into largest U.S. retailer; remained chairman up to his death

FRANCES WEAVER *(1928–)* U.S. writer and lecturer about aging's positive side. Attended college and began writing after husband's death; works include *The Girl with the Grandmother Faces* and *I'm Not As Old As I Used to Be*

FAY WELDON *(1933–)* English writer *(The Life and Loves of a She-Devil);* chiefly focuses on women's issues, often incorporating black humor and the supernatural

CAROLYN WELLS *(1869–1942)* U.S. writer of more than 170 mysteries, as well as children's books and light tall tales

JESSAMYN WEST *(1903–84)* U.S. writer for more than forty years; works such as *The Friendly Persuasion, Except for Me and Thee,* and *Cress Delahanty* sold more than 6 million copies

MAE WEST *(1892–1980)* U.S. actress, began in burlesque and vaudeville; best known for film roles she wrote or cowrote, all marked by sexual double entendres

BETTY WHITE *(1922–)* U.S. actress; produced and starred in first sitcom in 1952; acclaimed for work on *The Mary Tyler Moore Show* and *The Golden Girls;* animal-rights activist

STEWART EDWARD WHITE *(1873–1946)* U.S. writer; well known for novels set in California gold rush region as well as articles on nature

ELIE WIESEL *(1928–)* Romanian-born author and humanitarian; concentration camp survivor; author of thirty-six works focusing on the Holocaust, Judaism, and ethics; winner of Congressional Gold Medal of Achievement and the Nobel Prize for Peace

BILLY WILDER *(1906–)* Viennese-born U.S. film director, screenwriter, producer; acclaimed films include the Academy Award–winner *The Lost Weekend;* comedies, *The Apartment* and *Some Like it Hot*

WILLIAM CARLOS WILLIAMS *(1883–1963)* U.S. doctor and writer; celebrated the ordinary, the poor, and the working class in modernist works such as poem "The Red Wheelbarrow" and epic *Paterson;* winner of Pulitzer Prize and National Book Award

EDMUND WILSON *(1895–1972)* Influential U.S. literary critic, novelist, and social commentator; works include *Memoirs of Hecate County, To the Finland Station,* studies of symbolist and Civil War literature

ELLA WINTER *(1898–1980)* Australian journalist and social activist; focused her work on communist Russia; campaigned for migrant workers, unions, Jewish refugees, and Spanish loyalists

P. G. WODEHOUSE *(1881–1975)* English writer of humor novels and short stories, mostly spoofing English gentry

FRANK LLOYD WRIGHT *(1867–1959)* American architect with bold, innovative style; completed Guggenheim Museum in New York at age ninety-one

GENERAL CHARLES ELWOOD "CHUCK" YEAGER *(1923–)* U.S. test pilot; first human to break sound barrier; commander of the USAF Aerospace Research Pilot School

EDWARD YOUNG (1683–1765) English tragic and satiric poet *(The Love of Fame, the Universal Passion)*

HENNY YOUNGMAN *(1906–98)* American comedian and king of the one-liner ("Take my wife—please!"); spent seventy years in show biz, chiefly doing stand-up; averaged about two hundred dates a year